MW00814056

Dior

CATWALK

Dior

CATWALK

The Complete Collections

Introduction and designer profiles by Alexander Fury
Collection texts by Adélia Sabatini

With over 1,100 illustrations

Contents

The Collections

Christian Dior

Yves Saint Laurent

Marc Bohan

Gianfranco Ferré

John Galliano

Bill Gaytten

Raf Simons

The Studio

Maria Grazia Chiuri

Introduction

'Without foundations, there can be no fashion'

The true fashion moment is much mythologized, but seldom encountered. Despite the fashion industry's assertions to the contrary, there have been few. That is because the true fashion moment requires a tricky set of circumstances to materialize, to transmogrify a mere showing of clothes into something that galvanizes wider culture into taking note, resonating on a larger scale. The true fashion moment is about translating the ephemeral into material, about creating garments that express, somehow, the hopes and fears and aspirations of then and there. A fashion moment is often prophesied, but only a handful of fashion designers – even the greatest of the great – can lay claim to having achieved it.

Fashion's many proposed 'moments' are seldom pinned down as precisely as that which occurred on 12 February 1947, when a young couture house named after its founder, Christian Dior, debuted a spring haute couture collection in a Paris still gripped by winter. The house of Dior had been established less than two months earlier, financed by billionaire textile magnate Marcel Boussac, and envisaged by Dior from the very start as a small and exclusive house, devoted to clothes of *grand luxe*. Both the metaphorical *maison de couture* and the physical house itself at 30 avenue Montaigne had been readied at breakneck speed. The final bang of the final hammer was heard as the first clients and press entered the salons.

'I wanted a house in which every single thing would be new,' recalled Christian Dior, a decade later, in his autobiography *Dior by Dior*. 'From the ambiance and the staff, down to the furniture and even the address. All around us, life was beginning anew: it was time for a new trend in fashion.' The new was what Dior symbolized, for fashion generally and for Paris specifically. A new fashion, for a new era, sweeping away the austerity of wartime. Dior's clothes were shown in a salon freshly painted a gentle dove grey, its neoclassical décor a million miles from Gabrielle Chanel's honey-hued modernism on the rue Cambon or Elsa Schiaparelli's arresting Surrealist high jinks (shocking pink carpets, Salvador Dalí-installed window displays) in Place Vendôme. Dior's *cabine* of mannequins moved differently, too, with a graceful pirouetting walk, a delicacy. Dior was the home of the new.

The couturier himself did not have the temerity to call his clothes new. That came from the entranced editor-in-chief of America's *Harper's Bazaar*, Carmel Snow, who fêted Dior for dresses that had *such* a new look. But the collection Dior showed then – and there – was more than that. It was a revelation, a revolution, the supreme fashion moment. Ignoring the fashions of the recent past, Dior created something profoundly different: an impression of softness, of fragility, of *la femme fleur*, tightly fitted bodices like buds moulding a minute waist and emphatic bust and hips, the skirt below spreading like a flower, billowing to the mid-calf.

Carmel Snow was right. Everything about the collection was new. It erased the recent past. If shoulders had been square, Dior's were rounded; if shoes had been heavily platformed and hats high-piled with fruit, flowers and gewgaws, suddenly ankles were delicate, millinery streamlined. The abundance of fabric, more than anything else, epitomized a move away from the scrimping and saving, the making do and mending, that emblemized wartime strife. Dior's clothes looked towards a bright future. The key model of the collection? *Le Tailleur Bar*, a softly curved ivory silk tussore jacket, basques padded to set off a handspan midriff, above a skirt pleated from four metres of black wool. It formed an indelible image, one that still resonates with us today, seventy years later. *Le Bar* is representative, simultaneously, of femininity incarnate, of haute couture's supremacy, and of the power of fashion.

More than anything else, it looked *new*.

∴

Dior's fashion moment was the ultimate – the perfect fashion, perfectly timed. 'No man can surpass his own time,' said philosopher Georg Hegel, 'for the spirit of his time is also his own spirit.' The immediate, spectacular *succès fou* of Dior, and his fashion moment, can be traced to just that, to Dior's encapsulation of the hopes and dreams of an entire epoch, especially in Europe and specifically in Paris. Converse to the temporal nature of fashion – and certainly of fashion as era-defining as that couturier's debut – Dior's fashion moment has outlived itself, and even him.

Dior's debut was unprecedented, its influence unparalleled. No designer before, or since, has wielded so much power so immediately. 'Never in the history of fashion had a single designer made such a revolution in his first showing,' declared the normally reserved *Time* magazine, in March 1957, a decade after Dior's triumph and only six months before he died. That month, it put Dior on its cover – the first couturier ever thus featured. It cemented his stature, and global recognition.

The genius of Dior's New Look lay in his absolute certainty of what he was proposing – because, as Hegel states, his spirit was fused with that of his time. What Dior did, that was so new, was to offer a salve for a wounded world ripped apart by World War II, sweeping away still-lingering fears and restrictions. As he wrote in his autobiography: 'It happened that my own inclinations coincided with the tendency of the times and thus attained added importance... We were just emerging from a poverty-stricken, parsimonious era, obsessed with ration books and clothes-coupons: it was only natural that my creations should take the form of a reaction against this dearth of imagination… Europe was tired of dropping bombs and now only wanted to let off fireworks.'

Dior's medium was haute couture. Perhaps it would have had less impact if it had been art, against the prevailing Abstract Expressionism of Willem de Kooning and of Jackson Pollock, who began his radical 'drip' paintings the same year Dior debuted. That is because, despite its sobriquet, Dior's actual look wasn't about newness, other than in contrast to the prevailing trends of that epoch. It was about reminiscence and fantasy, about erasing the hardship of the present, by glancing back at the past. 'In December 1946, as a result of the war and uniforms, women still looked and dressed like Amazons,' Dior explained in his autobiography. 'I designed clothes for flower-like women.'

Dior's radicalism was rooted in nostalgia: his New Look revived techniques last seen in the Edwardian era, and silhouettes redolent of the Second Empire, when haute couture was first born at the hands of another man, Charles Frederick Worth. It also echoed the development of recent fashions: prior to the outbreak of war, couturiers had begun to experiment with styles derived from the nineteenth century, with wider skirts and corsets that pinched an hourglass waist, albeit under the era's signature, well-squared shoulders.

Dior himself, by 1937 designing for the house of Robert Piguet, created softly curvaceous styles with defined waists and wide skirts, foreshadowing the look that would make his name globally famous. An early design, named 'Café Anglais', saw a full-skirted *pied de poule* dress trimmed in lingerie lace, a combination of masculine textile and feminine shape, of tailoring and *flou*. It presaged not only Dior's 1947 debut, but his entire career. That Piguet dress was, of course, a success – just as those elements would be, again and again, under the label 'Christian Dior'. His later work, for Lucien Lelong, from 1941 until 1946, followed similar lines, his clothes sketching a silhouette around Lelong's clientele that seemed softer, more feminine. New.

Nevertheless, the impact of February 1947 – of Dior's particular fashion moment – cannot be underestimated. The press at the time lauded Dior. Laurels were heaped. 'What everyone now wanted from Paris,' gushed Bettina Ballard of American *Vogue*. 'A Napoleon, an Alexander the Great, a Caesar of the couture.' The succinct summary of her *Bazaar* contemporary, Carmel Snow? 'Dior saved Paris.' By 1956, notes writer and curator Alexandra Palmer, the house of Dior was responsible for generating half the total French haute couture exports to the USA, and by 1958 employed 1,500 people. *Time* magazine reported: '[Dior] is Atlas, holding up the entire French fashion industry.'

∴

If the true fashion moment is about rendering the intangible suddenly tangible, Christian Dior's enduring signatures are dual: on the one hand, concrete; on the other ideological. A silhouette versus a sensibility.

The Dior silhouette is solid, easily sketched, immediately recognized, comprised of narrow waist and full skirt, the form of *woman*. It remains embedded in the monochrome imagery of *Le Bar* and its bombastic, bombasted curvature, a shape emphatically carved through painstaking workmanship possible only through Parisian haute couture. Christian Dior once stated that his wish was to save women from nature: *Le Bar* emphasizes nature, but then exaggerates it, creating an idealized version of the female form, crafted by the hand of man.

The craft inherent in the creation of the Dior silhouette is another hallmark. Dior founded his house on the principles of returning to lost or overlooked skills – to the tradition of great luxury, to borrow his phrase. Dior gowns were akin to architecture or engineering; they were masterpieces of design. The specificity of each Dior creation emphasized the primacy of French know-how: even today, the techniques and craftspeople used to create Dior clothing can only be found in France, working for the haute couture. Since the 1960s, the challenge has been to translate that into ready-to-wear and accessories: John Galliano compared the haute couture to the *essence absolue*, or pure *parfum*, its potent strength and luxury informing the creativity of the multiple other lines that, today, form Dior's livelihood, just like *eau de parfum*.

Alongside the silhouette of *Le Bar* and the ateliers' superlative craftsmanship are other signifiers of Dior – subtle aesthetic clues, codes, that nevertheless unmistakably semaphore the identity of the house. Provocative hints of lingerie, of the déshabillé; the pairing of delicate lace with hardy wools; the use of masculine fabrics – flannels, tweeds, Prince of Wales checks – to contrast gloriously feminine shapes. Flowers, as prints, tucked into necklines or hemlines, or sublimated into the form of a gown that seems to grow organically around the body of a woman. And a palette: a strident geranium red, Dior's lucky colour; a pink that matched the rough-cast exterior of his childhood home in his birthplace of Granville; and a swelling symphony of greys, the colours Dior felt were most elegant in all of couture. Those greys recall the sea and sky of the Normandy coastline, where Granville is perched, but to Dior they were 'très Paris'. One shade of pearl-grey, still on the walls of avenue Montaigne, seems *changeant* in the Paris light: it has become so associated with the house that it has been christened 'Dior Grey'.

These codes, these unexpected emblems, this visual language of the house of Dior, have obsessed the couturier's successors from the eighties through until today – Gianfranco Ferré, John Galliano, Raf Simons, Maria Grazia Chiuri. Their job has been to tell a new story, with a new voice, but through the

vocabulary of Dior. They did not know Monsieur Dior intimately, like
Yves Saint Laurent or Marc Bohan – they inherited his mantle cold.
Their job, each season, has been to bring Dior back to life.

'I see us as guarders of his spirit, keepers of his dreams,' said John Galliano
in 2007, a decade after he took the reins of the *maison*. He was referring to
his predecessors, but his subsequent successors have approached Dior's
legacy in a similar way: Raf Simons referred to himself as a 'caretaker';
Maria Grazia Chiuri called herself a 'curator' when discussing her debut
ready-to-wear collection for spring/summer 2017, the start of a year of
celebrations marking the seventieth anniversary of Dior. Through each
of their collections, a thread of Dior can be seen, tracing his key silhouettes,
blushing Dior's choices of colour through the clothes. Perhaps that thread
is as effervescent as his fragrance, Diorissimo, heavy with the scent of
Dior's favourite flower, lily of the valley. He would tuck a sprig inside
the hems of his dresses, for good luck.

Dior was obsessed with superstition, with the immaterial, the intangible
and impalpable. He began his autobiography by eulogizing his good luck:
no major life decision was made without consulting clairvoyants, touching
wood and clutching at talismans. He believed passionately, and above all
else, in the power of fate. That is why, alongside the material legacy of Dior,
sits the cerebral and indefinable. The signature of Dior isn't just embedded
in the seams of his clothing, the factual, practical details of fabric, cut
and construction; it's embodied in an attitude, a certain psychology,
a state of mind.

Dior stands for romance, seduction, allure. All of these are open to
interpretation, and hence can be represented by various methods through
clothing. They can be evident in a billowing ball gown, as well as a sharply
cut trouser suit or a black leather jacket – all of which have appeared
under the name 'Christian Dior'. The easiest shorthand remains the
undulating lines of *Le Bar*, but those notions represent the *ideology* of Dior –
not the house's visual codes, but rather the thought process, the beliefs,
behind them.

That sensibility is the vital element in understanding the appeal of Dior
then, today and tomorrow. It is about more than a silhouette: it's about a
set of ideals, originally embedded in that silhouette but easily extracted.
That identity of Dior is present in John Galliano's sinuous bias-cut slip
dresses, in the mercurial fluidity of his tailoring, lightening Dior's
construction for modern clients; in Raf Simons's slick trouser suits, a brave
new vision of femininity for the twenty-first century; in Maria Grazia Chiuri's
fusion of femininity and feminism, of sportswear mixed with high fashion. It
is so quintessentially Dior, it has even crossed gender boundaries: when Hedi
Slimane established the Dior Homme line in 2000, it was by translating the
fundamentally female world of haute couture into a man's wardrobe, using

supple silks, featherlight construction, leather corsages crafted by the couture *plumassier* Lemarié. Even in Dior's masculine attire, the message resonates with the power of the eternally feminine.

∴

Fashion has fractured and fragmented since Dior's debut: no other designer could, single-handedly, affect the course of an entire industry and transform the way the world dressed, in their first collection or otherwise. Dior himself never achieved it again, although he worked for ten more years, establishing himself as an arbiter of taste for the world's women, and his reputation as 'the General Motors of the high fashion business'. Upon his death in 1957, the house of Dior's annual income was around $20 million. 'Fashion's ten-year wonder leaves couture leadership a question,' declared *The New York Times*, above reproductions of a litany of Dior lines, emphasizing the late couturier's grip on the decade. 'This plump, pink, shy man, the richest, most successful Parisian designer of all time, leaves behind him the world's biggest fashion empire,' it stated.

Since 1984, Bernard Arnault has helmed the Christian Dior business, reviving the house's fortunes in spectacular fashion and installing designers to steer the label. Each choice, bold and brave, has keyed Dior precisely to the dominant mood of the moment. They ensure the house leads, rather than follows. The challenge for those successors of Dior – there have been six named artistic directors in the sixty years since Monsieur Dior's death, alongside two year-long periods led by the studio – might be seen to be the same as that faced by Dior himself: living up to the New Look, to the fashion moment that exceeded them all. This, however, is not only impossible, but unnecessary.

The philosopher Walter Benjamin asserted that 'fashion is the eternal recurrence of the new'. And the history of Christian Dior is a history of revolution; of not just one 'New Look', but of thousands. Dior himself revolutionized fashion season after season through the forties and fifties, abandoning the New Look in favour of ambitious, architectural lines, transforming women biannually into different abstract shapes. After his death, under the direction of Yves Saint Laurent, the house had another triumph, another new look to hurrah; three years later, it was Marc Bohan's turn; in 1997, John Galliano's. And so on. Each of Dior's designers seeks to capture a speck of the magic that exploded on 12 February 1947, to do justice to the magical power of the name 'Christian Dior'.

Testament and key to their creativity is the platform of the runway show. Dior's earliest collections were presented in the crowded couture salons of 30 avenue Montaigne. As fashion's great trend-setter whose creations determined the course of contemporary fashion, Dior – the house, and the man – were terrified of copyists and restricted both attendance and documentation of these early shows, in line with the rules of the Chambre Syndicale de la Haute Couture, the governing body of the French fashion industry. Catwalk images are not always available for this period, hence some of the posed stills to be seen on these pages: fashion was more commonly represented by drawings in the popular press, and immortalized later by photographers such as Irving Penn or Richard Avedon. But as the runway show evolved into existence in the seventies and eighties, taking on ever-increasing importance and visibility, so the house of Dior kicked open the door to the salons. They rose to the challenge, staging some of the most awe-inspiring runway shows ever. For John Galliano's debut in 1997, the Grand Hotel was transformed into a facsimile of the Dior salons, albeit super-sized, draped with 800 metres of Dior grey fabric and adorned with 4,200 roses. In 2012, Raf Simons tasked Antwerp florist Mark Colle with decorating a series of salons in a grand *hôtel particulier* with over a million flowers – delphiniums, orchids, mimosa, roses – for his first Dior haute couture show. Dior has staged runway shows on Parisian steam trains, in sumo rings, and in the palaces of Blenheim and Versailles. The house's shows have redefined 'spectacular' when it comes to fashion. The only things that could upstage these shows were those clothes.

∴

Just as Gabrielle Chanel's designs have been acclaimed as a style, a 'look', rather than mere garments, so the work of Christian Dior is often seen as the apotheosis of fashion. The house's triumph is knotted up, inextricably, with a particular place and time, entirely emblematic of a moment in history – of a moment in fashion – and of a man who changed the way the world looked. We are told that fashions fade, but style is eternal. However, Dior – the ultimate fashion house, with the ultimate fashion statement – has confounded all expectations, bucked all trends, and transcended fashion. Seventy years after the spectacular debut of its genius founder, and sixty years after his death, the house of Christian Dior survives, indestructible. And so does the legacy of his 'New Look' – a fashion moment that, conversely, became eternal.

Alexander Fury

The Collections

Christian Dior

Looking To The New

A reluctant revolutionary, masterful businessman and astounding creative;
the man who wanted to make women dream again. Christian Dior – a magic
name Jean Cocteau dubbed 'of God and gold' (*Dieu* and *or*, in French) –
wrought seismic change in fashion. He re-established Paris's dominance of
the industry in the post-war cultural landscape; he asserted the unparalleled
excellence of haute couture against a rising tide of mass-manufacture; and,
of course, he transformed how women dressed. He did so from the very first
garments bearing the Dior label – his debut collection, for spring/summer
1947, a duo of lines which Dior himself dubbed '8' and 'Corolla', but which
history calls the 'New Look'.

Dior's life story has been frequently told, and much mythologized. He was
born on 21 January 1905, raised solidly bourgeois in Granville, a small town
on the Normandy coast in the northwest of France. His father, Maurice Dior,
headed the family firm, established two generations prior, manufacturing
fertilizer. His mother, born Marie Madeleine Juliette Martin, was a paragon
of elegance. Dior's childhood, however, had little to suggest the seeds of the
couturier he would become, bar an interest in clothing, a prodigious aptitude
for drawing and a wish to study art that was rebuked by his parents. Instead,
he was expected to follow the example of his uncle Lucien, a member of
parliament, and duly enrolled at the École des Sciences Politiques in Paris
in 1923. He would never complete his exams.

Instead, in 1928, Maurice Dior advanced his son several hundred thousand
francs to establish a fledgling art gallery, which supported Dalí, Giorgio
de Chirico and Picasso, among others. It closed in 1931. A second gallery
was opened in 1932, but shut in 1934, after the Great Depression decimated
the Dior family fortune. By the mid-thirties a penniless Dior had therefore
turned to the couture to earn money, initially selling sketches freelance,
then working for Robert Piguet and Lucien Lelong as designer. His work was
met with phenomenal success from the start: designs, by an unknown, that
were seized upon by houses eager to execute them, under their own name.
Dior's identity as the creator of the styles, however, began to become known.

In 1946, Dior met the textile magnate Marcel Boussac – the king of cotton, and the richest man in France – initially to discuss a proposition to revive a dusty house named Philippe et Gaston, now forgotten bar the role it plays in the Dior story. Christian Dior refused, unless the house was his own. On 16 December 1946, with backing from Boussac, the house of Christian Dior opened at 30 avenue Montaigne. Its debut would be at the spring/summer collections of 1947. The rest is history – a decade of dazzling innovation and experimentation under its founder, during which time the house of Dior rose to the very pinnacle of the fashion industry. That assertion isn't merely creative; it's also commercial. By 1949, Christian Dior accounted for 75 per cent of French fashion exports, and 5 per cent of France's exports total. The business was vast.

The New Look was Dior's greatest triumph. The evening following its spectacular unveiling, the artist Christian Bérard allegedly whispered: 'Tomorrow begins the anguish of living up to, and if possible surpassing, yourself.' Dior went on to present line after line that served to establish his supremacy in haute couture: the 'Spindle'; the 'Oblique'; and an alphabet of graphic shapes – 'A', 'Y', 'H'. He adored highly structured, complicated clothing. His collections were composed of dramatic, geometric silhouettes, generally achieved through elaborate underpinnings and tailoring techniques: Dior dresses, it was said, could stand up alone due to this formidable internal architecture. Yet, outside, Dior dresses were placid and stately – a contrast to the whip-crack speed of change between the lines, which came to define the notion of the ever-volatile fashion ideal, as opposed to the gentle evolution of decades prior. Dior was nostalgic in aesthetic, but decidedly forward-thinking in his fashion outlook.

When he died of a heart attack in 1957, after a decade of upheaval at his hands, Dior left not only a fashion empire bearing his name, but also a fashion industry imprinted with his impact. The triumph that he, in the end, could never surpass, has in turn never been exceeded by the talents that followed him. Dior remains the only man who truly made the world look new.

Alexander Fury

The 'New Look' ('Corolle' and '8' Lines)

On the morning of 12 February 1947, crowds gathered on Paris's avenue Montaigne for the last haute couture show of the season – that of the newly founded house of Christian Dior. *Vogue* editor Bettina Ballard, in attendance in the freshly painted grey salons, recalled being 'conscious of an electric tension that I had never before felt in couture'.

The unveiling of Dior's first collection lived up to the excitement. Ballard continued: 'The first girl came out, stepping fast, switching with a provocative swinging movement, whirling in the close-packed room, knocking over ashtrays with the strong flare of her pleated skirt, and bringing everyone to the edges of their seats in a desire not to miss a thread of this momentous occasion.'

Lasting over two hours (a Dior haute couture collection typically comprised over 200 designs) in spite of the models' rapid pace, the collection made headlines the world over. The Paris edition of the *New York Herald Tribune* called it the 'sensation of the season', although its greatest champion in the press was Carmel Snow, the editor of *Harper's Bazaar*, who declared 'it's quite a revolution, dear Christian. Your dresses have such a new look', coining the term that was to enter fashion history.

The original press notes for the collection (written by Christian Dior himself) described the two main silhouettes: the 'Corolle' (Corolla) line ('dance-like, very full-skirted, moulded bust and slim waist') and the '8' line ('clean and rounded, the chest is underlined, hollowed-out waist, accented hips').

'The lines of this first spring collection are typically feminine and designed to flatter the women who wear it,' Dior continued. 'Skirts are markedly longer, waists are clearly marked, jackets are often shortened – everything contributes to making the silhouette more slender.' The key colours were described as 'navy, grey, greige and black'.

Dior's first collection was an immense success and made the cover of American *Vogue*, which also photographed the iconic 'Bar' suit (opposite) for its Paris report. 'There were no "easy little dresses", no flashing theatrical designs. Rather, each model was constructed with a deep knowledge of dressmaking, to give you an exaggeratedly feminine figure, even if nature has not.'

'The opening of Christian Dior's new Paris couture house ... not only presented an extraordinarily beautiful collection; it gave the French couture a new assurance in its own abilities,' *Vogue* concluded.

'The New Look Pushed to Extremes'

'Dior has repeated his first success of five months ago,' *Vogue* proclaimed. 'His second collection proves that he is not just occasionally good. To characterize his collection: what is generally true of Paris design this season is particularly valid at Dior. The form is Dior's form.'

'Close bodice, practically padless shoulders, and yards of skirt' is how the magazine described the Dior silhouette, calling the new line (with 'the fall of the shoulder pad ... the important trappings under clothes: the built-in roundness, the built-in waist-corsets, and how they revamp the figure and rearrange the way a woman walks and sits') 'the most legible fashion change in over a decade'.

The original collection notes written by the house stressed the importance of 'soft shoulders, full busts, slim waists, rounded hips'. Two silhouettes were contrasted: 'stem woman or flower woman'. The former was expressed in 'the narrow silhouette profiled in the line baptised "*Derrière de Paris*"', and the latter through the 'Corolla silhouette', which here 'curves, flares into a tulip shape'.

'Take last season's round hipline, small shoulder, pulled-in waist, longer skirt, and emphasize each; stress the bosom, the *derrière*; add a side-moving hat, and you'll have a composite view of the Paris form for the new season,' *Vogue* reported.

Pleated 'petal panels' were inserted in long skirts, and there were several striking padded-out peplum jackets worn over tube skirts. Key accessories included 'side hats' ('it may be a beret, a pillbox, or toque – but it hugs one side of the head, completely bares the other side, where the hair is massed in a clump or a coil') and 'mammoth brilliants' as necklaces, *Vogue* added.

'It was a crazy collection of immensely wide, immensely long skirts, the New Look pushed to extremes,' Christian Dior later wrote in his autobiography, *Dior by Dior*. 'Dresses took up a fantastic yardage of material, and this time went right down to the ankles. Girls could safely feel that they had all the trappings of a fairy-tale princess to wear.'

'A golden age seemed to have come again,' the couturier continued. 'War had passed out of sight and there were no other wars on the horizon. What did the weight of my sumptuous materials, my heavy velvets and brocades, matter? When hearts were light, mere fabrics could not weigh the body down. Abundance was still too much of a novelty for a poverty cult to develop out of inverted snobbism.'

The 'Zig-Zag' & 'Envol' Lines

'In spring 1948 came the "Zig-Zag" line, which gave the figure the animated look of a drawing,' Christian Dior wrote in his autobiography. Alongside this 'Zig-Zag' silhouette, the new collection also introduced the 'Envol' ('Fly Away') line, characterized by 'a fullness that it distributed unequally, rising up when one walks and plunging towards the back,' according to the original show notes.

'At Dior,' *Vogue* wrote, 'skirt interest swung to the back.' The magazine also noted in its Paris report 'more focus below the waist, less emphasis on bosom' and 'more American shirtwaist dresses'.

Describing the collection as 'magnificent', *The New York Times* explained that 'fullness, instead of being the result of yardage as in the original corolle gowns, spreads stiffly like a tent, because fabric – smooth woollens, taffetas, natural shantung or supple dotted surahs – is backed by buckram or canvas as if pasted upon it'.

'Skirts, peplums, the backs of loose jackets and three-quarter coats flare in stiffened grace,' the newspaper continued. 'But in this versatile collection the slim gown has its place. The most sensational are street frocks, classical in front but with a stiffened wing protruding down the back, daringly at bustle height but tapering toward the hem.'

Eveningwear was also praised. 'The new lingerie evening gowns, both sheath and full, will make history this season ... lace insertion and Valenciennes ruching alternate from décolletage to hem, the whole over pale blue or pink satin foundation.'

The 'Ligne Ailée' (Winged Line)

Christian Dior explained in his autobiography that spring 1948 had brought the '"Zig-Zag" line, which gave the figure the animated look of a drawing'. Now, 'With winter, this tendency was confirmed by the "Winged" line. The silhouette had achieved its peak youth and flightiness.'

'The new collection is presented under the sign of WINGS,' declared the original collection notes. 'This season, interest is no longer in the length of the skirts, but in the cut and the repartition of the nervously drawn – no longer loose and undulating – volume.'

'Simple dresses and coats spread because of the weight of superb blanket cloths rather than excessive yardage,' reported *The New York Times*. 'Both have a single deep inverted pleat in back and front. Shortened to about fourteen inches, they have a youthful swing.'

The couturier 'adds the fantasy of stiffened detached yokes, flyaway boleros, high-pointed collars, and jutting cuffs to give a winged effect,' *The Observer* noted. 'To add a still greater look of movement he puts spiral drapery round his short dance dresses and calls this his "cyclone" effect'. A striking example of this new 'Cyclone' (or 'Hurricane') line is the 'Cyclone' dress in charcoal-black taffeta shown here (right).

Dior also introduced what *Vogue* described as 'slanting necklines' – 'drawn close over one shoulder, blown away from the other', as seen on 'Coquette', the pearl-grey satin 'great gala' dress shown overleaf (p. 34).

Evening dresses also featured dramatic, gravity-defying pleats. 'Stiffly flared skirts spread out at one side in wings that are like flattened cornucopias,' wrote *The New York Times*. 'So many are grouped together that they suggest the leaves of an open book. As the hemline of this group of wings is shorter than the rest of the skirt their lining of moire or satin can be glimpsed.'

The 'Trompe L'œil' Line

'There are two principles on which the "Trompe
L'œil" line is founded,' Christian Dior wrote. 'One is
to give the bust prominence and breadth, at the same
time respecting the natural curve of the shoulders;
the other principle leaves the body its natural line
but gives fullness and indispensable movement to
the skirts.'

'The "trompe l'œil" completely changes the cut
of the suit,' stated the collection notes. 'The very
spirit of the suits has changed. Instead of moulding
the bust, they have become suppler, even in the
traditional models. The bust fills out at the expense
of the basques, simple and without visible pockets.'

While there are few apparent pockets on suits, coats
and dresses, they are 'part of the line at Dior' and
used to create 'trompe l'œil' effects, Vogue wrote.
'There is the kangaroo pocket, pointed high above
the breast; the calla-lily pocket rising above the
shoulder; the pair of stiff silk pockets that form the
entire bodice of a dinner dress.'

Skirts also contributed to the optical illusions.
'Dior shortens perceptibly, by means of one or more
floating panels, and distributes an illusory fullness
asymmetrically about a stem skirt,' The New York
Times reported. 'At Dior, floating skirt-panels like
pleats, each pleat separately slit,' Vogue noted.
'Floating panels like Maypole ribbons, swinging
over narrow skirts. Circular panels like enormous
petals over skin-tight underskirts.'

For evening, 'among cocktail gowns are simple
chemise frocks in pink eyelet lawn, in white chiffon
with huge breast pockets, in gold and black lace,
in white pique fabulously embroidered in black
wool and rhinestones,' The New York Times added.
Gala gowns, suitably luxurious and dramatic,
are the only ensembles that are floor length.

The 'Milieu du Siècle' (Mid-Century) Collection

Baptised 'Mid-Century' (Milieu du Siècle), Dior's autumn/winter 1949–1950 collection 'does not depend upon the past for inspiration but takes its movement from the present,' the couturier told *The New York Times*.

'It was very expert,' Dior later wrote in his autobiography. 'It was founded on a system of cutting based on the internal geometry of the material. I have mentioned earlier the importance of the grain of the material: at this period, my models exploited it to the utmost.'

'Straight- and bias-cut intersect "like scissors" or radiate "like windmills" in a style that is purely of our time,' read the collection notes, and emphasize the way fabrics are contrasted: 'gros grain and velvet, velvet and wool, satin and velvet' (or, in the case of the 'Bâteleur' ensemble – shown opposite, top – black wool and fur).

'Scissors are at their best in evening gowns of slender sheath-like silhouette,' *The New York Times* reported. 'One, floor length, with bodice of black velvet, skirt of black broadcloth, had "scissors" forming two delicate panels of velvet crossing just below the belt and falling to the hem' (see opposite, bottom right).

There were also 'windmill drapes swirling to the side or back in a movement that is away from the tight sheath-like body of the dress,' the newspaper added. 'Collars and décolletage that have a dashing outward movement are also placed in this windmill category.'

'Large raised triangle-shaped collars frame the face and fall toward the back, revealing the nape of the neck – they're "windbreaker" collars,' explained the collection notes.

A number of coats and jackets were inspired by the loose shape of a shepherd's 'houppelande' cloak, 'a deliberately rugged and primitive style,' explained the notes, while ensembles were accessorized with André Perugia's asymmetric heels ('the asymmetric, and nakedest of shoes, to wear in contrast with bulky winter woollens,' *Vogue* wrote).

'Superb artistry dominates the Christian Dior collection,' *The New York Times* judged. 'From beginning to end – when a dress of fairy-tale beauty, its petaled skirt embroidered in jeweled beads the color of a dragonfly's wings, was shown [see 'Junon', p. 41] – this great couturier demonstrated his mastery of his materials. They follow his direction as the marble does a sculptor's hand and the colors a painter's brush.'

The 'Ligne Verticale'
(Vertical Line)

'The collection of spring 1950 saw the triumph of the vertical line, which put "woman" at a premium among women,' Christian Dior recalled in his autobiography. 'Busts were narrowly moulded, waists well nipped-in, and colours were clear like daylight.'

'Experts agree the biggest news in his fashion collection was Dior's treatment of the bust,' *The Washington Post* proclaimed. 'Large, round picture-collars framing the chest somewhat like a tuxedo or a horsecollar, showed off the bosom which was covered with a slightly opened or buttoned band of white or matching material.'

Suits were one of the key elements of the collection, with two main styles presented: tightly fitted jackets with stiff basques worn over 'apron' skirts (see opposite) and looser, 'vertical' box jackets worn over low-pleated skirts (right). 'Fitted jackets round out over the hips a little in front and have the featured "horseshoe" opening flanked by revers in the same shape, stiffened to be slightly convex,' *The New York Times* reported. 'Their slim skirts have a flat apron front rounded at the hem.'

After a nod to shepherds the previous season (see p. 38), the straighter and looser styles of short coats and jackets were inspired by 'the casual elegance of sailors and sailors' smocks,' the collection notes explained. The maritime theme also influenced the colour palette, with navy, white and black described as key tones.

'Spencer jackets and boleros disappear almost entirely,' the collection notes continued, replaced in part by silk duster coats such as 'Mascotte' shown overleaf (p. 44, top left).

'Most 1950, although they recall the early "Thirties" are bell skirts up in front but just touching the floor in back,' *The New York Times* noted. 'Iridescent paillettes or swirling rows of smallest pink Valencienne[s] make the entire gown.' Through his evening creations, Christian Dior set out to underline 'that quality of "work done by fairy fingers" which characterizes Parisian couture'. Dior 'returns also to the fine detail and fabulous workmanship legendary with the French couture,' echoed *The New York Times*.

'Length, volume, embroidery, shimmering fabrics – everything is inspired by a desire of fairytale-like transformation, which contrasts with the deliberate simplicity of day outfits,' stated the collection notes. 'We have given musicians' names to these dresses, which we have strived to make as immaterial as music' – see overleaf, for example, 'Mozart' (far right) and 'Liszt' (third from right) worn by house models surrounding Christian Dior after a special presentation of the collection at the Savoy hotel in London (p. 45, bottom).

The 'Ligne Oblique'
(Oblique Line)

After the vertical (see p. 42), Christian Dior baptised this collection the 'ligne oblique' (oblique line) – 'a more complex cut,' according to the collection notes compiled by the couturier himself.

Exemplified by the 'Embuscade' ensemble shown opposite, the key characteristics of the oblique line were listed as follows: 'small head; slender neck; sloped shoulders, widened bust; slim waist; ample basques and skirts'. 'Big, vertically placed pockets with deep flaps add to the hip importance,' *The New York Times* noted, while buttons often followed an oblique line.

There was also a series of high collars christened 'collets montés' by the couturier, and *Vogue* commented on 'Dior's collars... Large stiff cape collars on dresses, coats, or suits, sometimes turning into scarfs crossed and belted at the waist. Coats with great turned-up scarf collars covering the ears.'

The shirtwaist dress was entirely banished, but the couturier introduced both flared wool dresses (see 'Briquette', right) and, as the collection notes explained, 'a series of wide or narrow dresses entirely worked in oblique pleats that wrap around the body like a drape'.

'Most of the hats were small and set squarely over the brow,' *The New York Times* reported. 'Suits called for a modified homburg, with dresses and coats were cushion-brimmed toques, while long capes were accompanied by "nonnettes", closely fitted fabric caps with long scarf ends hanging at either side.'

Dior also introduced what he called the 'Dior chignon' ('a little rolled and twisted pyramid either of net or tulle ... placed directly above the forehead,' to quote *The New York Times*), which was worn by some of the models presenting after-dark ensembles (see p. 49).

'As for evening dresses, they expressed the desire for luxury, calm, happiness, and beauty, which was in the air,' Christian Dior later wrote in his autobiography. 'All are floor length,' the collection notes stated, and 'nothing is too sumptuous for them', with a lavish use of faille, satin and taffeta, as well as 'huge whirls of tulle and lace'.

The 'Ligne Naturelle'
(Natural Line)

Christian Dior's 'Ligne Naturelle' (Natural Line)
was built around one central theme: 'the oval'.
'Oval of the face, oval of the bust, oval of the hips:
these three superimposed ovals best express the
line of 1951, whose cut had to be entirely renewed
so as to follow the *natural* curves of the female
body,' the collection notes explained. 'Everything
is modelled on these subtle curves... Supple without
being loose, simple without being dry, the fashion
of 1951 is all about nuances.'

'Dior, who gave the padded, pleated New Look its
name, turned his back on all padding and stiffening,
and only used pleats when they were clinging like
fluted columns,' *Vogue* reported. 'He made carved
oval dresses with skirts you could walk in, because
he had added the slightest godets at the back, that
took nothing from slimness but gave all to comfort.'

'Dior's collection is built around grey, from oyster
to elephant,' Reuter noted. 'The silhouette is divided
into three ovals, the first is formed by long hair
brushed back and a down-curving hat, the second
by rounded shoulders with full sleeves, ending in
unexaggerated slimness at the waist, and the third
by a full-hipped skirt tapering slightly to the hem.'

Suits, jackets and dresses feature Dior's new
'cuisse de poulet' (chicken thigh) sleeves: 'sleeves
are set far into the front by a curved seam but
are in one piece with the back. Three quarters and
tapering into the forearm,' *The New York Times* wrote.

The newest jacket was a collarless 'paletot' –
'a box coat with Chinese ancestry,' *Vogue* wrote
(see opposite, top). 'Loose, hip length jackets
seemingly fuller under the arms than at the
hem are legion, in everything from beige tweed,
smooth gray, black or navy woolen to shantung.
Under these and upon strapped décolleté frocks
is worn a tight bolero just covering the bust in
length or a snug spencer with deep oval neckline,'
The New York Times reported. 'Keyhole necklines
are formed by a small band collar that merges
into the sides of a V or oval.'

Formal evening dresses, however, 'have a
deliberately different look and break absolutely
with the restraint and modesty that characterise
day ensembles,' the collection notes stated. 'They
borrow their names from the world of the theatre
because we have wanted to give them every flight
of fancy, daring and artifice.'

The 'Ligne Longue'
(Long Line)

'The oval [see p. 50] ... succeeded the oblique [see p. 46], and finally I introduced the "Long line", which was the favourite of all my collections,' Christian Dior wrote in his autobiography.

'From the hat to the shoes, it's a silhouette of entirely new proportions, which are a conclusion of the evolution started in the previous collection,' proclaimed the original collection notes. 'Trompe l'œil and artifices are out of date. Fashion is all about what is natural and sincere. The cut sculpts dresses and suits, dismisses ornaments.'

'Attention is focused on the supple and draped bust, from which two divergent lines – in seams or in darts – are drawn and, from the chest to the bottom of the noticeably lengthened skirt, give the body maximum slenderness: it's the *long* line.'

'Christian Dior lengthens skirts to cover the calf, shortens jacket peplums to four or five inches or less, thus further increasing the long look of the skirt. Moreover, skirts of measured fullness flaring ever so slightly, introduced tentatively in February, now predominate,' *The New York Times* reported.

'The high Directoire waistline is continuously suggested, by the high back belts, by taffeta coats with fullness gathered to a yoke, by smooth corselettes up to the bust on dresses though of course the natural waistline is always moulded, often princess. Likewise suggestive of a high waistline are boleros added to frocks from morning to evening.'

Ensembles were accessorized with new 'strong Cuban-heeled, soft-bowed pumps' created by Perugia for Dior, *Vogue* noted, while evening dresses were often worn with a bolero or a scarf and decorated with rich embroidery (contrasting with the more pared-back aesthetic of day suits and dresses).

The 'Ligne Sinueuse' (Sinuous Line)

'1952 was a serious year from the first – the year when the Iron Curtain was heavily clamped down, fires were lit in Indo-China and Korea, and Arab nationalism was reviving ... away with the euphoria of the New Look, and the fripperies of yesteryear. The new essential of fashion was that it should be discreet,' Christian Dior would later write in his autobiography.

'That is why in spring 1952 I proposed the "Sinuous" line; to indicate that fashion, for once logical, was succeeding the rigours of winter with a season of suppleness. Blouses and sweaters became the major theme of the collection, whose colours oscillated between natural and grey. At the same time, the waist became looser. The road towards the "Arrow" line [see p. 90] – which is the exact antithesis of the New Look – was opened up.'

The silhouette for this collection 'allowed the body complete freedom and movements all their ease,' the collection notes stated. 'Skirts, rarely narrow, flare out from the hips in a multitude of pleats that don't hinder walking.'

'Sweater dresses are in one piece, but with tops that continue to a band or cuff around the hips,' *The Washington Post* reported. 'Although there is no seam or belt at the waist, it is well marked and narrowed by darts', and the line follows the natural curves of the body.

'The sumptuous evening scene includes all silhouettes,' *The New York Times* noted. 'The moderate fullness in dirndls of embroidered organza, the strapless sweater bodice set to a skirt in tiers of fluted tulle, the bell skirts of taffeta or lace that are shorter in front but trail the floor in back, and, finally, sumptuous mid-Victorian crinolines.'

'Evening dresses to which two seasons earlier I had given the names of musicians [see p. 42] now bore the names of authors,' Christian Dior wrote. 'This nomenclature caused some curious conversations in the workrooms... In the *cabine*, a mannequin would exclaim crossly: "Look out! You're crushing Maurice Rostand," or "Don't trample on Albert Camus like that."'

The 'Ligne Profilée'
(Profile Line)

'In the autumn, the silhouette took inspiration
from modern techniques with the "Profile" line,'
Christian Dior wrote. This 'Ligne Profilée' was
inspired by 'the shapes modern life surrounds
us with', and owed its precision 'no longer to lines
but rather to natural curves refined and profiled
with care,' explained the collection notes.

'Dresses make the body slimmer without breaking
the silhouette and elongate it, as confirmed by the
length of the skirts, which are 10 centimetres longer
than the previous season... Wide or narrow, dresses
are profiled with the lively precision of planes or cars.
Moulded to the body, their goal is first and foremost
to thin down and lengthen.'

'Dior stands alone and strong for the profile line,
where moulded construction – plus higher necks,
longer skirts, slimmer unbroken waists – exaggerates
length of figure,' *Vogue* reported. 'The designing
of seams is like a lesson in the construction of a
beautiful building. His clothes do for figures what
few figures can do alone. He calls this the "profile"
line, and doesn't cling to one "profile" but outlines
many, all definitely, and generally in black... His
completely slim profile follows the curve of the
ideal body.'

'Dior calls the waistline "unbroken". It is never
cinched. There is no artificial emphasis anywhere.
The cut is so perfect, the look so custom-made
that description cannot do justice to the simplicity
of high tight collars, smooth long sleeves and
buttons down the center front,' *The New York
Times* echoed.

Richly embroidered evening dresses (which
would inspire Raf Simons and be transformed
into bustiers worn with black cigarette trousers
in his first collection for the house; see p. 528)
followed the same streamlined approach.

The 'Ligne Tulipe'
(Tulip Line)

In spring 1953, the 'Ligne Tulipe' (Tulip Line)
appeared, 'marked by the development of the
bust and the narrowing of the hips,' Christian Dior
later wrote in his autobiography. 'Little by little,
the waist was being freed', and this collection
would go on to directly inspire John Galliano's
own 'ligne florale' in 2010 (see p. 498).

'By masterful cut and manipulation of material
so that it stands away from the bust, Christian Dior
gives the bosom new emphasis, tailored yet supple,'
Dorothy Vernon wrote in *The New York Times*.
'He calls this schematic line the "open tulip".'

In suits particularly (see overleaf), 'the curve of
the tulip cut is just under the bust, then like the
petals the line spreads upward and outward to
the shoulders,' Vernon continued. 'The body from
the bust down is, of course, the tulip stem, and
a stem silhouette it is, princess lines following the
natural figure without particular emphasis on the
waistline and with hips effaced by jacket peplums
clinging to natural contours.'

The new line was amended, however, for 'dresses
with pleated skirts which, due to their fullness,
necessitate bodices of smaller proportions' (to
quote the collection notes) and whose top half
was therefore occasionally emphasized by other
means. 'In supple black silk and wool mixtures,
chiffon or crêpe prints, bust emphasis is given
by a draped fichu swathing the shoulders, and
crossed in front and back above a molded midriff
and stem skirt, with the exception of swirling
pleated prints that call for a flatter bodice with
shirt collar,' *The New York Times* reported.

'But the beauty of this collection depends not
only upon construction but upon fabric and
coloring: fresh yellowy spring greens, soft yellows,
rose-reds, rose, flower blue, basic black, beige and
gray, exquisite prints in blended impressionistic
patterns,' the newspaper added.

Colours drew on three themes, the collection
notes stated: 'prints inspired by the Impressionists
and evoking the fields of flowers dear to Renoir
and Van Gogh; prints whose colours and patterns
were borrowed from Persian miniatures [a motif
John Galliano would revisit in his collections
for the house; see, for example, pp. 310 and 478];
and, finally, great branches in bloom inspired
by China' (many years before Galliano's own
chinoiserie-themed creations; see p. 266).

The 'Ligne Vivante'
(Living Line)

'The Paris story this season turns round the tidal habit of skirt lengths – Dior, with no warning, shooting his up to just below the knee in a revolutionary collection inspired by the Paris skyline, Eiffel Tower for the slim number, Dome of the Invalides for the full,' *The Manchester Guardian* reported.

Baptised 'Ligne Vivante' (Living Line), Dior's new collection launched two new silhouettes: the 'Eiffel Tower' and the 'Cupolas of Paris' lines.

The 'Cupola' silhouette was most noticeable in dresses and coats. 'The dome dresses were all extremely simple, buttoning up to a round collar neckline. They had unpretentious short sleeves,' Dorothy Vernon noted in *The New York Times*. The couturier 'gives it that name because, from below a princess waistline, short gowns curve out over the hips in the rounded contours of a dome, in perfect smoothness and cut in six or eight gores.'

'When a coat just as short must cover such a rigid flare it becomes extremely wide in proportion to length,' Vernon pointed out, and *Vogue* featured Dior's 'cupola' coats ('rounded, bulky, one long curve from collar to hem') extensively in its pages that year.

'Eiffel Tower' dresses were narrower, spreading subtly from a princess waistline to the hemline. 'The proportions of slender gowns were also changed by the shortness,' *The New York Times* wrote. 'Princess, they buttoned down the back but in front gently molded the midriff up to a horizontal seam under the bust... Only the necklines differed, those for day being high, round and collarless, those for evening spreading to the shoulders in a wide V or low bateau.'

'I was always searching to alter the general attraction of woman and enliven her silhouette,' Christian Dior wrote. 'The material ought to *live* on her shoulders, and her figure *live* beneath the material' in a collection in which dresses were 'all about movement and life', the collection notes explained.

The couturier told The Associated Press that another 'revolution' had been overlooked in the frenzy and shock over shorter hemlines. 'For the first time I have done away with corsets, even for dance dresses,' he declared. 'I've also broken with waist seams, and cut my dresses in one piece, on princess lines. I've wanted to do away with belts for two years and now I've done it.'

This collection also marked the first time models wore shoes made by the newly founded firm of Christian Dior-Delman, created and directed by Roger Vivier.

The 'Ligne Muguet'
(Lily of the Valley Line)

'In the spring of 1954, I put forward the "Lily-of-the-Valley" line, inspired by my lucky flower, a line which was at once young, graceful and simple, and which was given unity by its colour: Paris blue,' the couturier explained in his autobiography.

'The lily of the valley ingredient refers to the over-all inspiration: head volume given by flat hats, with a cushion of fabric for crowns; softly bloused bodice, belted waists, soft skirts evoking, according to M. Dior, the descending flowerlets of this tender spring flower,' Phyllis Heathcote wrote for *The Manchester Guardian*.

'The new fashion says goodbye to the princess line [see p. 66] and sails towards new adventures,' proclaimed the collection notes. 'Young, supple and simple like the flower that symbolizes it', the new spring look favoured easy 'luncheon-to-dinner' ensembles for modern women.

'Without change in skirt length, Christian Dior has abandoned princess lines for a supple silhouette based on the shirt frock with a sailor collar and blousing slightly over a non-shaped belt as round as a ring,' *The New York Times* reported. 'Adding to the soft look of bloused bodices in print chiffon are separate draped fichus and artists' ties that swing down into cowl drapery at the back.'

Blue was the star colour in this collection, alongside black, grey, white, lilac and 'petunia' pink. Prints and embroidery motifs were inspired by flowers, gardens, orchards and branches in bloom, and decorated everything from matching hat and dress prints for day to richly embroidered evening dresses.

Of his company, the designer noted in his autobiography: 'Christian Dior now reached the age of reason and celebrated his seventh birthday. He now occupied five buildings, included twenty-eight workrooms and employed more than a thousand persons.'

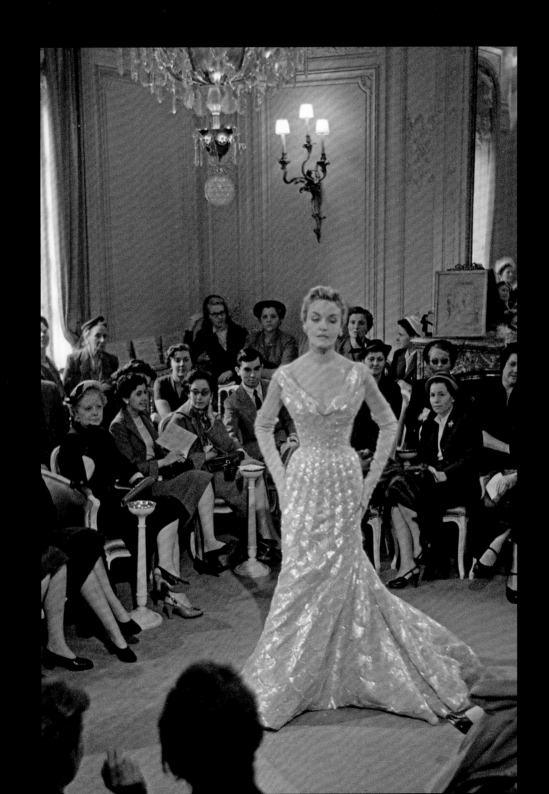

The 'H' Line

Described as a 'Silhouette Hanchée' (hip-based silhouette) in the original collection notes, the H-line was defined by the couturier as 'an entirely different line, based on the lengthening and the shrinking of the bust: it is on those parallels forming the tall letter H that dresses, suits and coats are built'.

With garments cut high and loose on the chest, and draping, pockets or belts placed under the waist, right at the top of the hips, Dior achieved 'this effect of a long bust resting on the hips, which is the defining feature of the season'.

'If one were to find an analogy in the past for the slender body of today's woman,' he wrote, 'it would be the body of the nymphs of the School of Fontainebleau – the H of Henri II', the king who ruled France 400 years earlier (1547–59) and whose court at Fontainebleau castle welcomed artists such as François Clouet (who captured the beauty ideals of the time on his canvas, painting slim, high-chested, aristocratic beauties – perhaps most famously the king's mistress, Diane de Poitiers).

'The same love of style and purity. The same love of elegance and elongation. The same love of reserve and youth,' wrote Dior, linking 1555 to 1955.

Artistic parallels continued in the dainty shoes' new 'Watteau heel' and in the couturier's choice of colours: bright 'Vermeer blue' for day, a greyer 'Fontainebleau blue' and 'pure Vermeer yellow' for evening, plus reds and pinks that 'match the shades of the house's new lipsticks'.

'The H line marked the final evolution begun in 1952 [see p. 56] by the liberation of the waist,' Christian Dior would later declare in his autobiography. 'Almost immediately the new line was baptized the "Flat Look"; but it had never been my intention to create a flat fashion which would evoke the idea of a runner bean.'

Vogue concurred, arguing in its Paris report that 'Dior, far from flattening the bosom, has flattered it; has raised it, rounded it, given it an alluring look of youth' and praised 'the new statuesque evening line at Dior', exemplified by ensembles such as 'Zaïre' (opposite) and 'Amadis' (p. 80, left).

Finally, 'a salvo of bravos burst forth when the last dress, an enchanting bridal creation [see p. 81], came into the Dior showroom... There were cries of "divine" for this was unquestionably the best collection Christian Dior has made since his first of new look fame,' The New York Times reported.

The 'A' Line

'The rigours of winter and the parallels of the
H-line [see p. 74] are superseded in this spring's
silhouette by a line which is freer and more flared,'
announced the collection notes. 'It is perfectly
illustrated by the letter A, very similar in
construction to the letter H, but whose main
characteristic is the *inflection* of the *two diagonals*.
The angle between the two lends itself to an
infinity of variations.'

'In short there is a perceptible *evolution*, but
not a *revolution*, of the general silhouette whose
possibilities are far from being exhausted,' the
collection notes continued. 'If the bust still
seems to be lengthened, and that is the main
characteristic, the cross-bar of the A is in its
essence mobile, although the loose-fitting and
lightly marked waist remains in its natural
position without too much emphasis...
Play on the waist is one of the most important
points in this spring's fashion, and it is as
temperamental as the season itself.'

'There are many *basques*, and *belts* – the ideal
cross-bars of the A which is the symbol of the
collection', and 'typical wear for the daytime
is the jacket-dress ensemble,' according to the
collection notes. 'The A-line jacket spreads
from narrow shoulders to fingertip hemline.
Side buttoning points up the silhouette,'
The New York Times noted. 'A pleated skirt
or one with lampshade flare continues the
outward slant of the side of A.'

The A line was carried through evening
creations (shown overleaf as part of a fashion
show held for charity in Scotland a few months
after the collection was first presented in Paris),
which featured many short and ankle-length
evening gowns as well as rich embroideries.
'We have never made such a great use of them
before,' stated the collection notes. 'The simplicity
of the lines of evening dresses is perfectly suited
to the sumptuousness which they add. As discreet
as they are magnificent, they find their theme
in India just as easily as at the Trianon.'

'Enchanting Empire evening dresses are made
in several layers of silk organdie and for their
only trimmings have a ribbon lying under
the breasts. Others sprigged with flowers and
shimmering with gold and silver embroidery,
have the airy grace, the begotten not made,
look of Botticelli's Venus,' *The Manchester
Guardian* reported, while *Vogue* praised 'Dior's
white organdie mounted on satin' as 'Dior's
A line at its most delicate – and the prettiest
triangle since Pythagoras'.

The 'Y' Line

'Once again a letter of the alphabet, Y this time, which expresses the essential character of the new collection,' explained the original show notes. 'It is the sign of a *reaction* against long basques, low waists that are too loose-fitting and hats that are not really hats. It is a proof of the *evolution* that could be foreseen in the last collection [see p. 82] where play on the waist tended to make it narrower and higher and to put the accent on the bust which is emphasised by almost all the artifices of cutting.'

'The *high* bust opens out between the limbs of the Y which reach the base of the shoulders which are natural and small. A new way of setting the armholes is intended to define this line more clearly. The waist, which has been slimmed rather than squeezed, remains in its natural position, but has a tendency to be a little high, so skirts, and therefore the lower limbs of the Y, are of maximum length.'

'This desire to give fullness is also shown in the use of *loose-fitting coats* and *jackets* of every size with a preference for short jackets like "requimpettes" which makes day-dresses and spencers suitable for town-wear. This tendency is confirmed by the appearance of wide buttoned scarves with dress-coats which are fairly common' (see, for example, 'Kirghiz' right, and 'Voyageur' opposite).

'There is very little transition between very plain unsophisticated *town-wear* on the one hand and *long* or *short evening dresses* on the other. The latter, while taking up the themes of today's fashion, add every kind of fantasy, especially as regards skirts. With the exception of a few which are pleated, *all skirts* are narrow for day-wear, and they only recover their fullness at the end of the day; they then have the new "parachute" fullness which is sometimes considerable' (see p. 89, bottom).

'Short evening dresses are a good deal shorter than they were last season' and 'numerous faille skirts are *gathered into puffs, tucked up, hooked up,* or *swell out* in Turkish style,' added the collection notes. 'The oriental feeling in Paris this season rises to a peak at Dior's,' *The New York Times* reported. 'This is reflected in mandarin coat tunics with slit sides, fan pleated panels starting from under the arm, and coolie tunics buttoning down the back or side back.'

'All Dior hats are worn low on the forehead, some even touching the eyebrows. There are feather toques, berets, tambourines, oriental turbans, Persian bonnets, and flat plateau hats with undulating brims,' the newspaper added.

The 'Ligne Flèche' (Arrow Line)

'With the momentum of last season, the new collection darts like an arrow to its goal: high waist and arrow-like arm-holes,' announced the show notes for the collection baptised 'Ligne Flèche' (Arrow Line).

'The set of the sleeves – a straight line from the neck to the bottom of the sleeve – caps the straight silhouette with two obliques, while a trick of cutting, a fold or drape, a half-belt or belt, hollows out the profile into an f just below the bosom. F, the first letter of *femininity* and *flèche* (arrow) stands for soft curves and also for tall slenderness.'

'The *loose jacket* plays the lead this season, for the princess dress has given way to a dress consisting of two pieces: a *skirt* and a *loose jacket*. It allies severity and suppleness and is adapted to every hour of the day and to every occasion.'

'The suit caresses the waist, which is intentionally high, rather than emphasising it. *Basques* are a little *longer*, and the shawl, claudine or tailored collars are well away from the neck. What gives the suits an entirely new line are the sleeves and the loose-fitting cut of the back.'

'Still keeping to the same general principle, fullness in dresses for cocktail and evening wear starts right at the waist, which is sometimes high, and spreads out very wide. Fullness is always with the thread of the cloth and never on the bias,' the collection notes continued.

Vogue praised Dior's new 'caraco' jacket ('waist length, it folds above a belt for a look as soft as a blouse') and the new silhouette of the house: 'placed very high, and tied over fullness – this is the new Dior line that's creating an important place in spring fashion for the softly lifted waistline'.

'Belts are much more numerous than last season and play an important role, which is not to constrict the waist but to show it is high. They harmonize with the folds of dresses and are often tied with a knot,' the collection notes pointed out.

As for evening clothes, one of the key trends was 'the long unbroken sheath starting from a high empire waistline,' *The Washington Post* noted. 'It is lovely in vaporous sheers and rigid all-embroidered bell skirted gowns suggesting the shape of a pear. Floating panels attached high at the back pick up like a stole, enveloping the shoulders and arms, as the mannequins float through the salons' (see p. 93).

The 'Ligne Aimant'
(Magnet Line)

'A *Magnet* is what we first think of when we see the
line of the majority of models in this new Collection,'
proclaimed the show notes that accompanied the
presentation of Dior's 'Ligne Aimant' (Magnet Line).

'*Hats* have a high rounded crown and are close-fitting
at the temples. *Busts* are also rounded, whereas the
waist is rather more fitted. *Skirts* are full at the hips
and become narrower further down. The *Magnet* is
in effect the leitmotiv which reappears throughout
the Collection.'

'[M. Dior] uses the term "magnet" literally and
bases his new silhouette on its horseshoe shape,
the curved top forming the shoulder line, the
rounded sides corresponding to the curved hipline
and the narrow tips to the slender hemline,' *The New
York Times* reported, while the *New York Herald Tribune*'s
Eugenia Sheppard suggested, 'If you draw three
horseshoe-shaped magnets, one on top of the other,
with the smallest on the top, you'll get an idea
of the shape'.

'The set of the sleeves is absolutely new,' the
collection notes continued. 'They are set far back
and sometimes form what is really a yoke in the
back, rounding off the shoulders into a *Magnet*,
though the breadth across the shoulders is not
over-emphasised.'

'The other novelty in suits is the skirt. Sheath
skirts have almost disappeared. Wide or narrow,
set in the *Dutch* fashion, they are nearly all full
at the hips below the shortened basques.'

'Together with suits come an infinity of coats and
capes of every size and shape, sometimes intermediary
between the two. *Capes are one of the outstanding novelties
of the season*... Loose-fitting coats also adopt this *cape*
style, and adapt it in various ways,' the show notes
explained.

In majority short or ankle-length, evening dresses
contrasted with the day ensembles that preceded
them. 'Dior's daytime clothes are just as bulky and
cover-up as his evening clothes are bare,' remarked
Eugenia Sheppard. 'For dinner clothes, Dior revives
the most ravishing neckline in the world. Dresses
look as if they were clutched on just before they slip
off the shoulders. They have long tight sleeves and
are worn with velvet picture hats or sailors made
of black tulle.'

Key colours were '*black black* and *black and white*,'
the house announced. 'This season the dark grey
of the *Magnet* is more popular than browns which
take on lichen tones sometimes varying between
maroon and greenish.'

The 'Ligne Libre'
(Free Line)

'Exactly ten years ago Christian Dior skyrocketed into the world of fashion with his "New Look". Fame, in these intervening years, has neither altered his disposition nor impaired his talent. It was with a delightful smile that he said at the end of the showing, "This year I have altered the tone of my collection. It is by far the youngest and freshest I have ever designed. More than ever before, we need happiness and gaiety in our lives and I have tried to fulfil this need today", *The New York Times* reported.

'This season fashion has deliberately chosen freedom,' proclaimed the programme notes to a collection that had been baptised 'Ligne Libre' (Free Line). '*Freedom* in necklines, which stand more or less far away from the neck. *Freedom* in the waistline, around which the fabric "screws" itself loosely or a loose belt is buckled. *Freedom* in skirts which, whether wide or narrow, give the impression of volume... *Freedom* in lengths, which are essentially variable according to the time of day and the model.'

'The daytime dress is first and foremost a town dress, usually a two-piece comprising a "Vareuse" (Sailor's Jersey) and a skirt, which can be worn out-of-doors like a suit,' the collection notes continued. Skirts 'sometimes have a noticeable tendency to be long, especially sheath skirts; they are almost always slit over an underskirt, thus allowing complete freedom of movement', while 'for the end of the afternoon, sheath skirts have a tendency to become longer, sometimes dropping right down to the ankle'.

Vogue also singled out the house's slit sheaths (dubbed 'robes de Chine') for late day and evening. 'Two designers, Dior and Lanvin-Castillo, chose themes Oriental in origin but contemporary Occidental in effect.'

'Every couture house in Paris has ravishing white evening dresses,' *Vogue* continued in its report on the Paris collections. 'At Dior there is, in addition to his *robes chinoises*, a mildly narrow dress of white organdie bands, with a white doubled organdie scarf-wrap reaching to the floor ... there is a dotted net dress in white with a fichu to the waist, a full skirt just to the ankles; worn with it, bright pink slippers and a little white bow in the hair just above the forehead' (see opposite).

A number of evening dresses featured a short train (see p. 100, for example), while formal gala gowns included the floor-length 'Espagne' dress (shown p. 101) in white organdie with gold-embroidered flounces admired by Ingrid Bergman (who would go on to wear Dior in the 1958 film *Indiscreet*, directed by Stanley Donen).

The 'Ligne Fuseau' (Spindle Line)

The 'Ligne Fuseau' (Spindle Line) was to be Christian Dior's last collection for his eponymous house, before his unexpected death a few months later.

'The new silhouette for the day can so to speak be inscribed within the two brackets () of the *spindle* line,' the collection notes explained. 'Encased within these two curves, this line owes its elegance above all to its lengthening effect, which is compensated by a slight shortening of skirts.'

'[Suits] are deliberately loose fitting, but their line nevertheless follows the lines of the bust and is hollowed out below the bosom. The back remains straight,' the collection notes continued.

'Long-waisted blouses and hobble skirts for day were reminiscent of the flapper era,' *The Washington Post* wrote. 'Even Pola Negri would have felt at home in a number of the beaded, fringed evening sheaths', such as 'Calypso' (the short evening dress shown on p. 104 that would be worn by Jayne Mansfield, present in the audience on p. 105).

'Except for a few models which follow the same line as during the day, end-of-day dresses ... adopt quite a different style inspired by the 18th century,' the collection notes added. 'The bust is closely fitted, and its cut leads to a long waist effect. Bouffant skirts. With their bows, ruches, underskirts and becoming décolletés, they are in complete contrast with day fashion which is very plain if not austere.'

'The most fun [dresses] were the snug topped, stiffly bell-skirted ones. M. Dior's inspiration here came from the 18th century French court beauties such as Marie Antoinette, Madame du Barry, and Madame de Pompadour,' *The New York Times* reported. 'The necklines were something to behold. Gasps went up from the audience more than once. It's incredible how many new variations on the daring neckline Dior thought up.'

Vogue also picked up on what it called 'Dior extremes', contrasting '1920s Figure Masking' ('the Dior unwaisted look') with 'The Century Exposure' (dresses 'cut to a new degree of décolletage').

'In this new collection, Mr Dior presents both facets of his brilliant talent: one, his painter-architect mastery of abstract design; the other, his gift for making women look completely feminine (the basis of his great success in 1947),' wrote *Vogue* editor Jessica Daves. 'The new collection is one of extremes – of insistently unfitted dresses, coats, suits; of insistently fitted torso[s] ... with skirts blowing in a little cloud. And throughout, there is the unflagging professional perfection that explains, in part, the continuing Dior eminence.'

Yves Saint Laurent

Radical Chic

When Christian Dior died, aged 52, in October 1957, France was plunged into mourning and the house of Dior into crisis. Who could continue the legacy of the great man? Who was up to the job?

On 15 November 1957, the answer came: Yves Henri Donat Mathieu-Saint-Laurent, a former assistant, at the tender age of just 21. He seemed slight and unprepared for the weight of the role – but, unbeknownst to the world, many of the later creations under the name Dior had already come from his hands (35 in the autumn/winter 1957 collection, more than any single Dior assistant had created previously). In hindsight, those designs – notably the chemise – are characterized by a youthful verve and light construction, albeit still in the vein of the founder. They underline the style of a couturier whose name was soon snipped to merely Yves Saint Laurent, the better to underline his role as the chosen one, a saviour with God-given talent.

That was precisely the hyperbolic verdict that thundered after his debut collection for Christian Dior in January 1958: 'Yves Saint Laurent has saved France,' proclaimed *Le Figaro*, adding their voice to a chorus lauding a line Saint Laurent dubbed the 'Trapeze', a riff on his well-received chemise dresses of a season prior. He prepared the collection, he said, 'in a complete state of elation. I knew I was going to be famous.'

Yves Saint Laurent was born in Oran in Algeria in 1936. His father owned a chain of cinemas and the family were well-off bourgeoisie, with considerable society connections. Saint Laurent was doted on by his mother Lucienne, conspicuously well-dressed herself, and she encouraged her son's interest in the arts. Originally, he wanted to be a theatrical designer, but gradually grew more interested in the couture, creating sketches and designing dresses for his mother and sisters. In 1954, aged 17, he visited Paris and met Michel de Brunhoff, editor-in-chief of French *Vogue*, who encouraged Saint Laurent's talent. The next year, after his baccalaureate, he moved to Paris to study at the Chambre Syndicale. The same year, he won three of seven prizes in the prestigious International Wool Secretariat competition, aged just 18.

In January 1955, on the recommendation of de Brunhoff, who was impressed by the similarity between Saint Laurent's sketches and the as-yet-unveiled 'A' line, Dior offered him a job. Yves Saint Laurent was still only 18.

Precocious and prodigiously talented, Yves Saint Laurent set out on a career that was made by Dior. He quickly began to chafe, however, at the restrictions of the respectable haute couture house and the expectations of its clientele, radically altering lengths and silhouettes against a tacit rule of the fashion industry never to move hemlines more than two inches in a single season. If Dior had one New Look, Saint Laurent brought a revolution every season. In retrospect, his constant invention is thrilling, his imagination extraordinarily febrile. In practice, it was unsettling for both the industry at large and the house and its clients.

While Christian Dior's greatest achievement – and success – came precisely from reacting to the times, Saint Laurent was a fashion prophet. His autumn/winter 1960 'Beat' collection not only presaged the sixties short-skirted, straight-silhouetted lines; it was also the first instance of a high fashion house taking inspiration from youth subculture. Saint Laurent reflected a profound change in the fashion psyche, indicative of the 'Youthquake' that would restructure fashion during the next decade, making it unrecognizable to traditional couturiers. Dior's young designer had not just seen the future; he showed it to the rest of the world, in the hallowed salons of Christian Dior.

It proved too controversial, too loaded, for the house. Yves Saint Laurent was called up for 27 months of military service in September 1960, which, after repeated deferments, it was determined could be avoided no longer. There was conjecture as to whether Saint Laurent would provide sketches for Dior 'from the barracks', but after only nineteen days the couturier-cum-cadet was sent to Bégin Military Hospital on the outskirts of Paris, suffering a nervous collapse. Later in the same month, Marc Bohan was announced as his replacement.

Alexander Fury

The 'Ligne Trapèze'
(Trapeze Line)

Yves Saint Laurent's first collection for Dior,
the innovative 'Trapeze' line, was dedicated
to the late Christian Dior. 'You will understand
the emotion with which we present our collection
this morning,' a voice declared over loudspeakers
before the show. 'This one, and all those that
follow, will stand as a permanent homage to
the man who founded our house.'

Facing enormous pressure ('He'll Be Gambling
With $17 Million,' *The Washington Post* had headlined),
Saint Laurent delivered a collection that was a hit
with press and buyers alike. 'Rarely does a hoped-for
miracle come off just on time and in full splendor,
but it can happen,' *The New York Times* wrote.
'Younger than springtime, today's magnificent
collection has made a French national hero of
Dior's successor, 22-year-old Yves Saint Laurent
and comfortably assures the future of the house
that Dior built.'

'Fashion this season is a question of *balance*
and of *cut*,' read the original collection notes.
'The *balance* of a hat placed straight on the head,
the *balance* of the silhouette inserting itself in
the base of the *trapeze*.'

'The two most important points of the season
are: a) the *shoulders* on which rest the head of the
trapeze; b) the *fullness of the skirt* forming the base
of the trapeze.'

'This new construction of the silhouette brings
with it a very distinct shortening of the dresses',
of which there were two types: the 'two-piece'
(the superimposing of two trapezes, leaving the
waist free) and the 'blouse' (likened to a 'dress coat',
whose cut 'is balanced entirely on the shoulders').

Finally, for evening there were 'bouffant dresses,
decorated, beribboned, flowered, evoking ballerinas
and the operas dear to [Venetian painter Pietro]
Longhi', decorated with 'light, scintillating
embroidery'.

The 'Ligne Courbe – Silhouette en Arc' (Curved Line – Arched Silhouette)

Titled 'Curved Line – Arched Silhouette' ('Ligne Courbe – Silhouette en Arc'), Yves Saint Laurent's second collection for the house was architectural in spirit: after the trapeze (see p. 108), curves and arches.

'The structure of this season's fashions is inspired by one of the fundamental lines of architecture,' stated the collection notes, which described the 'curved convex line of hats closely framing the face, [the] definitive curve of the well-marked rounded shoulder line, [the] softened curves of skirts [and] the semi-circle of Palladio's arcades' as key characteristics.

'Straight and angular lines form hollows, spread out, curve and reveal the full and spectacular blossoming of the bust,' the notes continued. 'This line is a complete reaction from that of the last collection: a new "arched" cut and a new length (14 inches from the ground) give the silhouette unaccustomed proportions. Although the waist is short there is nothing *Directoire* about it. To find an analogy in the past, one must think of the women of Pisanello, Carpaccio and the Venetian painters of the Italian Renaissance.'

'What M. St. Laurent sets out to do,' wrote *Vogue* editor Jessica Daves, 'is to elongate the whole feminine figure by means of high heels, narrow shoes, narrow skirts, tall hats *and* the higher waistline. This proportion is the newest look in Paris.'

For day, there were dome-like coat dresses with 'draped collars with scarf or shawl effect, sometimes opening over a double skirt', while for evening the designer presented 'Period dresses, usually ankle length, recalling the Venice of the Renaissance and its grandeur, the Turkish styles of the 18th century, Goya', alongside splendid 'Baroque dresses' ('panache and parade dresses trimmed with ruching, ribbon loops, silk fringes … accompanied by masks or "velvet eyes"'), the collection notes explained.

After being shown in Paris (right), the collection was transported to Blenheim Palace for a special presentation in aid of the British Red Cross (see opposite and overleaf), as Christian Dior had done in 1954 for his H Line (and many decades before the house would return to Blenheim Palace for a special cruise collection; see p. 600).

Held on 12 November 1958, the event was attended by Princess Margaret (a faithful Dior client), who declared that she had 'never seen so beautiful a collection'. '1,650 women looked with leisured enchantment at something that seemed to evolve from a ballet, so lovely are the movements of the model girls in their rich clothes,' *The Observer* reported.

The 'Ligne Longue – Silhouette Naturelle' (Long Line – Natural Silhouette)

'No longer confined within the limits of a purely geometrical figure or the obligatory curve of an arch, this season, the silhouette is liberated,' read the original notes for the collection Yves Saint Laurent baptized 'Long Line – Natural Silhouette' ('Ligne Longue – Silhouette Naturelle').

'A new woman is born: *long*, extremely *long*, *supple, natural, easy,* suggested by the long *oblique* of the back and the *sinuous* line of the bust in its right place, of the supple waist, the subdued hips... A new chapter opens: *"No longer a new line but a new style"* – a style that sets out to be deliberately young, light-hearted, typically 1959.'

For day, Saint Laurent proposed easy tailored suits cinched at the waist (sometimes with large chiffon belts in contrasting colours), and delicate pleats allowing skirts and dresses to move freely. For evening, there were supple long sheath dresses in light satin, chiffon, crepe and shantung, alongside 'short evening dresses, extremely light, in a new style: dancing skirts, filmy or pleated collars ... with madly wide skirts, like a ballerina's'.

The new Dior woman was 'long in line, with none of the previous architectural construction surrounding her,' Saint Laurent told *The Washington Post.* 'At Dior, delicious and apparently uncontrived clothes,' *Vogue* reported; 'one looks twice to see the cunning and skill that have gone into their apparent effortlessness. The flutter of pleats and chiffon, deep berthas on pleated dresses; suits of pale shantung belted over sleeveless dresses; coats pulled in at the waist by belts or tied sashes – the look very like an elegant schoolgirl's'.

'1960'

'1960 – the surge of modern life has created a
new woman,' the show notes for this collection
proclaimed, arguing the need for a 'new fashion',
a 'new woman', a 'new attitude' and 'new basics'
– 'new trends realising what could be called:
1960 style'.

The newest – and most shocking – element
of the collection was a series of skirts baring the
knee, described by the house as 'the leitmotiv of
the collection'. 'The secret of my silhouette is in
the skirt and the way it is worked,' Saint Laurent
declared.

'Dior left the fashion press gasping with
amazement this morning,' *The New York Times*
wrote. 'Yves Saint Laurent was busy taking
up hems ... while everyone else was letting them
down. Sometimes, he even exposed at least the
front of a shapely knee. Actually, his biggest news
was a skirt that gathered at the waist and bloused
slightly over the top of a six-inch band at the hem,
giving the impression of a puffed tunic.'

The effect – if not the length – was replicated
in sumptuous formal evening gowns: 'many of
these, reminiscent of Paul Poiret styles, had skirt
widths gathered at knee level into a tight band
from which descended a flounce split up to the
knee in front and swooping to a small fish tail
train at the back,' *The Times* reported.

Featuring 'Dior's pouf-skirted suit' and 'Dior's
soufflé tunic' in the pages of her Paris report,
Vogue editor Jessica Daves judged the collection
'the most French collection in Paris'. 'It was
presented with superb, luxurious panache, and
much of it was shown on Victoire [right, wearing
'Coquine'], the famous Dior mannequin who, even
in this diminishing world, could never be mistaken
for anything but a Parisienne.'

The 'Silhouette de Demain' (Silhouette of Tomorrow)

'Today the great house of Dior showed a collection that is already being acclaimed as one of the most beautiful, spectacular and youthful that the house has ever introduced,' stated *The New York Times*.

The princess silhouette (particularly developed by Givenchy the previous season) was a key component of this collection, entitled 'The Silhouette of Tomorrow' ('Silhouette de Demain'), adapted here by Yves Saint Laurent in his own way and rendered in luminous colours.

'Coats go over two-piece dresses that look like divinely fitted middies and skirts. Some of them are in the same bright colour as the coats,' Eugenia Sheppard wrote for *The Washington Post*. 'The Dior collection also has a princess suit with a wrist length jacket that is shaped and flared.'

Accessorized with matching cylindrical hats (described by *Vogue* as 'domed melon-like fez'), Saint Laurent's creations for day featured high round necklines, from which 'the silhouettes ... spread out in pear, tent or doll-dress shapes to knee-high hemlines,' *The New York Times* reported.

'The big news in Dior dresses is the lack of sleeves. If there are any at all, they are kimono sleeves, ending at the elbow,' the newspaper added. 'Like every other Paris couturier St Laurent has a version of the two-piece tunic dress. His are the most extreme and the most fluid of all. The tunic tops have simple oval or bateau necklines and cling to the bosom only in front, while fluttering away like capes everywhere else. Under these are skirts that stick out too – tent on top of tent.'

'St Laurent too has been caught up in the business of putting women in glamorous pants for entertaining at home,' *The New York Times* continued. 'At one point, the salon was filled with mannequins, each one attired in either tight pants worn under overskirts or the most fetching peignoirs ever.'

Evening dresses were no less striking, with high waists and asymmetrical hems. 'St Laurent's evening sheath, short in front and with a long square train is for the girls who drink their whisky straight and coffee black,' Sheppard wrote. 'Some fragile flower print chiffons with floating, ruffle edged backs are for the crème de menthe crowd.'

'Souplesse, Légèreté, Vie' (Suppleness, Lightness, Liveliness)

'Dior has abandoned the waist, elongated the torso and shifted the emphasis of the silhouette to well below the hips in a most provocative collection shown this morning,' *The New York Times* reported on what was to be Yves Saint Laurent's last collection for the house, baptized 'Suppleness, Lightness, Liveliness' ('Souplesse, Légèreté, Vie'). 'The proportion is simply this: two parts for the torso and one part for the skirt', which was slightly puffed or balloon-shaped, while jackets and bodices were kept austerely simple with high collarless necklines and bare armholes.

'Clothes are fluid. Construction, something St Laurent has been throwing away each season, is definitely out of the window. Fabrics glide along the body,' *The New York Times* added. After bright colours the previous season (see p. 124), however, this time black was dominant.

'The beat look is the news at Dior ... pale zombie faces; leather suits and coats; knitted caps and high turtleneck collars, black endlessly,' British *Vogue* wrote. And indeed Saint Laurent seemed to have taken inspiration from his contemporaries, young artists and creatives, naming an ensemble in the collection 'A Bout de Souffle' (Jean-Luc Godard's film of the same name – *Breathless* in English – having been released a few months earlier), and another 'Aimez-vous Brahms' (after the eponymous novel by Françoise Sagan, then in her twenties, published in 1959), both black.

'Dior would like [women] to be avant-garde shapes in his own abstract designs – when they're not looking like schoolgirls in knitted caps and suits with knitted turtle-neck collars,' American *Vogue* editor Jessica Daves stated in her Paris report.

Fur was also present in the collection, but treated in unexpected ways: teamed with knitted sleeves or collars, used to trim leather jackets (in the iconic 'Chicago', a glossy black crocodile leather jacket edged with mink and tied with crocodile bows) or turned into the most luxurious of casual outfits (such as 'Television', an 'at-home' pull-over of white mink worked in horizontal bands worn with long black velvet trousers).

'To give a more sporting effect, he tops his girls with knitted bonnets shaped like acorns,' Phyllis Heathcote wrote for *The Guardian*. 'And that's not all. Jackets have knitted sleeves and fur coats, too. A leopard one, yes, that was amusing, but what can be said for knitted sleeves with mink!'

Marc Bohan

The Custodian

After the storm, the calm. Following the fireworks of Christian Dior and his near-constant shifts of hemline and silhouette, then the radical styles proposed by his successor Yves Saint Laurent, Marc Bohan's time at the house was marked by a quiet classicism, by gradual development of styles, by consistency.

That was exactly what Dior needed. Saint Laurent's youthful exuberance and constant transformations of style had unsettled department store buyers and private clients, who had, ironically, come to regard Dior as a safe investment, rather than a drastic fashion innovator; the press had also reacted with increasing hostility to Saint Laurent's attempts to reflect a changing society through haute couture clothing. By contrast, Bohan moved with the times but did not invent them. His tenure proved the longest of all, including that of Monsieur Dior: Bohan headed the house for 29 years, from 1960 through to 1989.

Unlike his predecessors and successors at Dior, there is scant information on Bohan's life and background, other than what can be assembled from contemporary articles and accounts. He was born in Paris in 1926. His mother was a milliner, who encouraged Bohan's own interest in fashion. After his graduation in 1944, he worked as a clerk at the Banque de Paris, but would sneak into couture shows during his lunch break. Then, in 1945, he began work at the house of Robert Piguet, echoing Christian Dior's own trajectory. In 1949, he moved to Molyneux, whose styles Dior himself admired immensely. Bohan attempted to establish his own house in 1953, but it closed after six months due to poor financing. He moved to the house of Jean Patou as chief designer in 1954, then in 1957 travelled to work in America. There, Christian Dior asked him to head his New York operation – producing ready-to-wear clothes for a local clientele, adapting lines determined by Paris. Dior died before the plan could be put into action, and already-emerging tensions between Bohan and Saint Laurent ultimately resulted in the plan stalling in 1958, despite press announcements. Bohan moved to head Dior's London operation, then, when Saint Laurent was drafted for military service in 1960, Bohan was appointed artistic director. Saint Laurent turned 24 in 1960 – Bohan was a decade older. He had worked in haute couture for sixteen years, versus Saint Laurent's scant four. The general consensus was that Dior was in safe hands.

Bohan's path at Dior was ultimately far more complicated than could ever have been imagined – but, if his talent fell short of Yves Saint Laurent's genius, his resilience and consistency were precisely what was required to inspire confidence in the house. He steered Dior through the seismic shifts that uprooted contemporary fashion during the sixties and seventies – foremost, the rise of designer ready-to-wear to become the dominant fashion force. Until the seventies, the bulk of couture's profits were made from department stores and mass-manufacturers purchasing the right to copy Paris originals, with varying degrees of verisimilitude and in varying quantities. Designer ready-to-wear changed that, affixing designer names – and cachet – to mass-produced clothes, and injecting them with as much creative impact as their couture antecedents. By the mid-seventies, it was the dominant influence, and a commercial giant. It was Yves Saint Laurent's Rive Gauche line that pioneered the concept in 1966 – but Bohan and Dior weren't far behind, launching a range of ready-to-wear labelled 'Miss Dior' in 1967. Menswear was added in 1970, while Dior's cosmetics empire was founded in 1969. Fragrances, including the first for men, Eau Sauvage (1966), and 1985's Poison, achieved remarkable success.

'N'oubliez pas la femme' – 'Don't forget the woman' – Bohan told Vogue in 1963. He never did. Alongside expanded lines and licensing agreements, Bohan retained a loyal cadre of devoted couture clients, including Elizabeth Taylor, Sophia Loren, and Princess Grace of Monaco, whose daughter, Princess Caroline, wed industrialist Philippe Junot in a dress he designed in 1978. Indeed, when Bohan departed Dior in 1989, he was credited with maintaining the largest number of clients for the made-to-measure haute couture in Paris. What were those women drawn to? The workmanship synonymous with Dior, and the inherent classicism of Bohan's brand of faultless chic.

Alexander Fury

The 'Slim Look'

'Thundering applause, led by the Duchess of
Windsor, rolled through the elegant grey-and-white
salons of the House of Dior, the happy ending
to the suspense story of the fashion year. At stake
was the future dominance of Dior and the career
of designer Marc Bohan – "Mister Dior, the third",
taking over from ailing Yves Saint Laurent,'
announced the *Chicago Tribune*.

'The shouting, clapping, surging mob at the
press showing caused chaos in the elegant salon,'
The New York Times added. 'M. Bohan was pushed
up against the boiserie, kissed, mauled, and
congratulated. Chairs were toppled. Champagne
glasses were broken. People were knocked down.
It was a complete triumph for the designer.'

For his first collection as head designer, Bohan
presented what he called the 'Slim Look': a simple,
supple, young and streamlined style – his modern
take on the original 'New Look'. The designer
revisited the day suit, with wide-cut jackets
and low-waisted, gently flared skirts closely fitted
to the hips and paired with Roger Vivier's iconic
curved 'comma-heel' shoes. Dramatic volume was
confined to the designer's 'globe' coats and dresses
(see p. 136, top).

'The garden party chiffons, worn with garden
party hats of coloured baku, entered four at a clip
to bravos and sighs of pure joy from the assembly,'
Vogue reported, while for evening Bohan presented
flared 'Slim Look' embroidered sheath dresses
in organdie, tulle or chiffon. The striking 'Hyménée'
wedding dress (see p. 137) closed the collection.

Bohan 'started out with the same inspiration
that has influenced most Paris designers this
season: the late 1920s,' *The New York Times* reported.
'His clothes underplayed the bosom. He dropped
the waistline to the hips and flared out the
short skirt.'

Acclaimed by the press – *The Times* declared
it 'a success from the appearance of the first
model, and worthily in the tradition of the great
maestro himself' – the 'Slim Look' was a hit.
Three months after the collection was first shown,
Women's Wear Daily wrote, 'The Bohan flare is
everywhere. Bohan has done the impossible:
he is a big commercial success and respected
by the fashion intellectuals.'

'Charm 62'

'Supple, sinuous and mobile' is how the
press notes described this collection, baptized
'Charm 62'. 'A neat head, slim shoulders, a high
bust, lengthened torso, flat hips. Skirts have
either wide gores and ripple out or are straight,
just standing away slightly at knee-level hemline',
in keeping with the 'Bohan flare' the designer
introduced at Dior the previous season (see p. 132).

The 'Slim Look' continued in the cut of
the suits: 'glove sleeves are long and narrow;
basques short'. They are 'often worn with
extra-short fur-lined cloaks, sometimes hooded,
or with "vareuses" fitting closely over the bust
and then widening in a cone effect'.

The hoods, cowls and muffled-up collars in
the collection caught the eye of *Vogue*, which
informed its readers that 'the greatest difference
is in the look of the head – the newest look,
Dior's tiny calot cap, like a glorified beanie,
with hair smoothly waved outside – beguiling,
unsevere, neat as the Persian princess's rose'.

One of the collection's most striking outfits
– a long evening dress of pink moiré with
matching stole (see opposite, captured in a
special presentation held for the Fashion Group
International, as were later Bohan collections) –
was photographed by Irving Penn for the
magazine, which described the collection
as 'huge, glittering, luxurious and beautiful'.
'The evening fabrics were glorious brocades,
velvets, beaded and furred, pink moire looking
mild as milk and unexpectedly delightful in
the midst of the dark velvet sable-lined coats...
The evening clothes, in a word, a television
word, were spectaculars,' *Vogue* concluded.

'Lightness, Suppleness, Femininity'

'Lightness, Suppleness, Femininity' – such
were the characteristics of this season's
creations, according to the collection notes.
'The style is free and very easy, but in no way
careless, and there is a fine subtlety in its details.'

'Shoulders are normal, torsos slender and
lengthened to the utmost; hips are rounded.
Skirts with single or multiple "facets" stop just
below the knee where the calf starts its curve,'
the house stated. Blouses were cut in woollen suit
fabric for day and teamed with contrasting suits.

Bohan's trademark flare was still present, with
coats 'fitted away from the body flaring gently
in an unbroken line' and evening dresses featuring
'an elongated bust and skirt with back fullness',
such as the green sheath (opposite, right) that
was captured by William Klein in the pages
of *Vogue* ('Dior's exacting green crêpe sheath –
only for the slender,' the magazine warned).

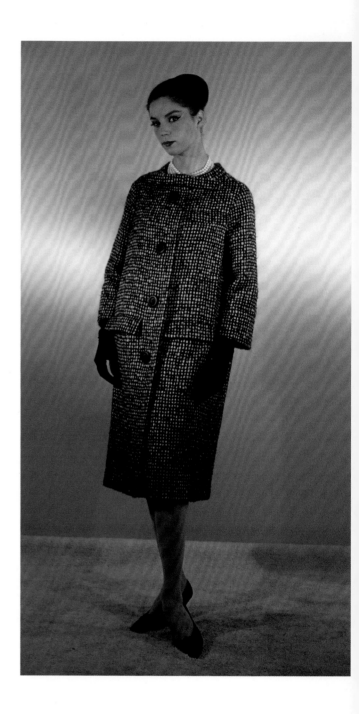

'Ligne Flèche'
(Arrow Line)

Baptized 'Ligne Flèche' (Arrow Line) in an echo of Christian Dior's 1956 collection of the same name (see p. 90), Marc Bohan's latest creations were designed for the new, jet-setting Dior woman who shoots across the world all year round, hopping from one continent to the next.

'A designer must not find himself at a loss when dealing with the sudden changes of climate that air travel brings, nor by the fact that sports no longer depend upon the season, since blue skies are within easy flying distance,' stated the collection notes.

'Impressed by the modification which has taken place in home life, with its small cocktail and television parties, Mr Bohan felt that he should think ahead for women of elegance and present them with a whole new series of town clothes, travel outfits, weekend wear suitable for sport or shooting parties and a wide selection of informal home attire.'

Ensembles were given suitably globetrotting names, from 'Air France' to 'Noël à Palm Beach' (Christmas in Palm Beach), 'Paris Tokyo', 'Saint Sylvestre à Rio' (New Year's Eve in Rio) and 'Soirée à Bangkok' (Evening in Bangkok).

Characterized by 'rounded shoulders, busts given proper emphasis, waists always noted, [and] slim hips', Bohan's 'arrow line' focused on a lengthened silhouette. His evening sheaths, in particular – embroidered or fur-trimmed – featured 'lifted' waists to 'enhance the bust and lengthen the legs, which are often glimpsed through opening panels or transparent fabrics' and were accessorized with 'oriental jewelry in enamel and gold and precious stones'.

'Tapered Silhouette'

Baptized 'Tapered Silhouette' (or 'Ligne Effilée'),
this collection was centred on the bust, echoing
the high, slender bust line of the designer's
creations the previous season (see p. 142).

It set out to present 'sinuous lines flowing in
a single stream from the shoulder hollow, exactly
where the rounded sleeve fits in near the neckline,'
according to the collection notes. 'Long darts
outline the silhouette, while the waistline is
revealed by the subtlety of movement. Super-
wide armholes highlight the bust line.'

Brightly coloured suits with 'short, easy jackets'
were offset by dramatic hats – 'huge, perfect circles
of light or plaited straw [to] frame the face with
a gay and precious radiance' – while evening
dresses were embroidered with multicoloured,
'high relief' floral motifs.

'Fashion, like today's way of life, is an evolution,'
proclaimed the collection notes. 'Rapid no doubt,
but logical. It is no longer a revolution. No longer
does it call for sudden, almost brutal changes
in the silhouette. More and more, the silhouette
is a matter of elegance of cut, subtlety of detail
and design.'

Squared Shoulders

For this new collection, Marc Bohan chose
to accentuate shoulder width, alongside 'high
necklines, importance given to collars and
décolletage, supple busts, belted waists [and a]
length for winter: hemline just below the knee,'
stated the collection notes. 'Sleeves are clean-set
and stress the square shoulder line.'

'Marc Bohan sent his models trotting out today
with the broad, padded shoulders of a high-fashion
football team,' Patricia Peterson wrote for *The New
York Times*, praising the use of 'some of the most
exciting tweeds in town in woody tones and
pastels' in the designer's day clothes.

Hailing 'the new Dior shoulder line squared
by two seams perched on the shoulders,' *Vogue*
reported on 'doubled necklines, many high
turnover turtlenecks' and 'above all: helmets,
medium-high, with flat bands, worn – like all
Paris hats – straight across the eyebrows'.

Evening dresses were 'fluid and lengthened
by a lifted waist' (in keeping with the designer's
previous collections), with 'either high necklines
or low, square decolletage', and were accompanied
by formal ball gowns with 'fine, precise, sculptured
outlines,' the house explained.

'The New Way of Life'

'Fashion cannot allow itself to remain static.
It has the obligation, even, to be one beat
ahead in the rhythm of modern existence and
to integrate itself into the "new way of life",' the
house proclaimed to introduce a contemporary
– and relatively daring – haute couture collection,
which was praised by *The New York Times* as
'triumphantly young ... sporty and easy to live in'.

'For travelling or cruising, for home or town,
in every climate and latitude, whatever the change
of place or tempo, the most exacting care in the
choice of fabrics and accessories and in every detail
contributes to that pursuit of femininity and charm
evident in the Spring '64 line,' read the show notes.

Featuring 'triangle collars, pointed décolletages ...
[and] mobile pleated skirts', the collection also
proposed comfortable 'envelope coats' ('geometric
and strict with raglan fit') and 'a new line of
"characterful and luxurious" clothes: jackets
and trousers for air travel, outfits for cocktails
at yachting parties and on cruises' with a more
relaxed fit.

According to *Vogue*, the star of the collection,
however, was the creation baptized 'Tom Jones'
(see right) – 'Marc Bohan's navy-blue crêpe late-day
dress ... one of the sensations of his collection
for Dior – inspired by the rollicky English movie'
[the 1963 adaptation of Henry Fielding's classic
novel, directed by Tony Richardson], which the
magazine described as 'the most talked about dress
in Paris'. 'Spirits are high in "Tom", but necklines
are low, and so is this – daringly low and wide,'
Vogue continued. 'Long, poetically full sleeves
with a small white gardenia caught at one wrist;
the skirt, all accordion pleats, breezy and spirited
in motion.'

'Pyramid' Suits
& Tube Dresses

'Dior: delightful, practical, luxurious,' judged
Vogue editor Diana Vreeland in her report on
the Paris collections. Defined by 'a more supple
shoulder line with raglan cut, a long bust, double
rows of buttoning widely spaced, romantic details'
and 'wide skirts gathered peasant-style', according
to the show notes, the collection also proposed
'tube dresses ... with deep, pointed décolletages
and long sleeves', '"moujik blouses" in lamé, chiffon,
crepe and velvet, sometimes fur-bordered', and
'"Rococo dresses" ... embroidered with jet'.

Vogue praised the two contrasting lines in the
collection, hailing 'Marc Bohan's double-barreled
suit-success for Dior: the ample, very moving
pyramids [vs] narrow-bodied shapes'.

The designer's 'stormy-day pyramid suit in
charcoal poplin with a woolly sweater belted
into culottes; flashes of patent-lightning...;
shoes like chopped boots, cut below the anklebone'
(right) was photographed by Irving Penn for the
magazine, as were examples of 'Dior's narrow look
– shaped to the body but not touching ... small
perfect shoulders ... narrow wristbone sleeves on
quick little coats; on proper city suits with high-
buttoned jackets chopped short over easy skirts'.

The star material was chenille, the house
stated, 'used in knitwear, embroidery, trimmings
and very often for whole garments'. 'One of the
prettiest alliances,' *The New York Times* reported,
'involved a taupe chenille jacket – which looked
as though someone's doting grandmother had
just finished crocheting it – over a deep-hipped,
full skirted satin dress in stinging pink'
(opposite, top right).

Headscarves accessorized a series of outfits,
'fringed or not, in the same fabric as the suit,'
the collection notes pointed out.

'The Mysterious Orient'

Marc Bohan embraced an Oriental mood
for this collection, which featured a series of
pared-back tunic dresses 'pale as the insides
of shells' (as *Vogue* described them), knee-length
for day and long for evening, such as the pale
pink crepe tunic and hobbled skirt printed with
large white flowers shown opposite, centre.

Floral motifs turned multicoloured on 'Hindoustan'
(see opposite, top right), the crepe creation *Vogue*
hailed as 'sensational ... a narrowed caftan draped
at the hem ... the Compagnie des Indes print,
jade green, Bristol blue, and pink on white ...
very like a 17th-century cotton' with 'tiny fake-
emerald buttons' down the front.

Suits were not forgotten, be they collarless with
small sleeves and tight armholes, or more amply
cut in wool or knitted jersey with belts, stripes
and pleats at the front, and accessorized with
pussy-bow scarves.

'The most beautiful collection was Bohan's for
Dior,' proclaimed *The New York Times*, commenting
on 'the mysterious Orient of turbans and fluid
dresses [that] influenced many couturiers'
that season.

Feathered Knits

Defined by a 'profiled silhouette, new supple
hangs, a long and stretched out bust … and easy
skirts', Marc Bohan's latest collection for the house
innovated with the introduction of a new material:
a wool fabric specially woven with feathers,
which was used in ensembles such as 'Pintade'
(pictured right).

'Feathers drop all over the collection, but don't
land on the predictable places,' wrote Gloria
Emerson for *The New York Times*. 'A gray wool
suit has an overblouse of plumes made from
guinea hen. A beige wool cardigan coat, round
and curvy, is covered with partridge feathers.'

Vogue's Diana Vreeland noted 'this new proportion
at Dior: wide-brimmed soft felt hats worn with
small narrow-shouldered suits'. The large hats,
inspired by the 17th-century Dutch painter
Frans Hals, were teamed with jackets featuring
'big, schoolgirl bows under tidy collars,' *The New
York Times* added, interpreting the dramatic
headpieces as 'the first sign that big hats
are making a comeback'.

Embroideries were strongly textured, with jet and
marcasite, and evening dresses featured intricate
back bows, folds and pleats – 'just as sexy: the
looperoos of Dior – dresses with a soft pannier
of looped fullness flung to the back, caught at
the nape of the neck or the waist,' *Vogue* reported.

'In a Mexican Mood'

'Dior is in a Mexican mood,' *The New York Times* headlined its report on the collection inspired by Marc Bohan's recent trip to Mexico and one of the designer's most colourful yet. 'Fuchsia is the preferred colour,' read the collection notes, 'and appears throughout the collection, accompanied by acid green, intense yellow, bright pink and deep purple.'

'Prints, all exclusive and Mexico-themed, are in shantung or chiffon' and show 'large motifs in violent and contrasted colours,' the house stated. The most striking examples of these fabrics, created by Brossin de Méré, were Bohan's evening pyjamas (see opposite, bottom right), described by *Vogue* as 'a flamboyant circus of colour, loosed in one voluminous chiffon spill, [which] overflows the body with the extravagance of Pierrot pantaloons'.

Reminiscent of the hand-painted and tie-dyed 'Goa' dresses that John Galliano would create for Dior decades later (see p. 349), Marc Bohan's brightly coloured silk evening pyjamas so caught the eye of *Vogue*'s editors that they reappeared in the magazine shortly after the Paris collection reports, shot by Richard Avedon and worn this time by a young Barbra Streisand.

Hats were another highlight – decorated with 'Mexican prints' or made out of unusual materials such as 'wood, cork, or plastic' in dramatic shapes, the show notes explained. There were also 'off-the-shoulder necklines copied from Mexican blouses,' *The New York Times* noted.

Military Coats
& Slashed Shoulders

'Greatcoats with long skirts that hide the tops
of boots marched out today in Marc Bohan's winter
collection for Christian Dior,' *The New York Times*
reported. 'Under the coats, tween the uniforms
of Czarist troops and West Point cadets, are ladylike
suits or dresses... Bohan calls them "tin soldier"
outfits because his ankle-length coats have epaulets,
brass buttons, high half-belts or wide leather
ones with square buckles that were inspired by
sword belts.'

There were 'suits with supple jackets, following the
body's contour' that had 'no collars, and sometimes
only one lapel is turned down,' stated the show notes,
while blouses were '"tee shirts" in brilliant coloured
crepe, contrasting with woollen suit fabrics'.

'The long trumpet sleeve from the last Dior
collection [see p. 156] is back again,' *The New York
Times* noted, 'but now Bohan has slashed it so deeply
it splits open at the elbow. There is a Dior cutout,
too: a peekaboo slit baring the shoulder [with] big
rhinestone balls at each end of the split.'

For evening, there were 'long, supple dresses,
straight or flared, in black or brightly-coloured
crepe, worn with "Nanny" capes or long woollen
coats', as well as delicate 'long "gandura" [tunics]
in transparent lace worn over scintillating sheaths,'
the house stated.

'African Style'

Decades before John Galliano's Maasai–Dior
silhouette (see p. 260) and his Africa-influenced
collection (see p. 470), Marc Bohan looked to the
African continent for inspiration in this haute
couture collection.

The designer presented two types of suit: the
'Safari' suit ('with elongated jackets and patch
pockets') and the 'short-jacketed, shirt-collar suit',
both teamed with 'Safari' felt hats, the collection
notes stated.

For evening, there were 'African Style' prints,
'Totem-dresses' ('either caught on to plastron
neckpieces or embroidered with native designs'),
'Boubou-dresses' ('asymmetrical, with one shoulder
bared, in crepe, shantung or multi-coloured gauze
or even in white embroidered organdie or patterned
feathers'), 'Creeper-dresses' ('clinging to the body
and featuring amulet chain belts or asymmetrical
embroidery'), 'Explorer outfits' ('worn with battle
type jackets in "Virgin Forest" printed crepe and
curb-chain belts') and 'Bermuda-dresses' ('long-
skirted, in plain or printed crepe for dancing').

Accessories were in keeping with the collection's
theme, from 'amulet' or 'seed' belts to wooden
buttons ('the newest detail: a yoke attached
to the body of a dress by lacquered nuts, gold
crescents or gold balls,' noted *The New York
Times*) and 'African style' embroideries ('wooden,
tortoiseshell and gold paillettes in Totem
designs or wild, motley-coloured African masks,'
the house explained).

'Romantic Style'

With its 'cravat collars; jabots; lace, fringe or feather cuffs [and] high necklines', Marc Bohan's latest collection focused on 'Romantic Style', the show notes explained (an aesthetic John Galliano would revisit in his own Romantic collections, see pp. 496 and 512).

With a 'supple and belted' silhouette and a hemline that stopped just above the knee, the collection was accessorized with 'wide, hip-level military belts with round, transparent buckles in tortoiseshell or black lacquer', wide-brimmed black felt hats or 'clerical' hats ('*chapeaux d'abbé*') with 'shallow crowns and curled up brims', and black patent leather shoes.

For day, Bohan presented series of what *Vogue* described as 'Dior's stable-boy coats', alongside 'short, close-fitting jackets with patch pockets and round collars [worn] over supple, flared skirts, occasionally box-pleated,' the collection notes stated. There were also 'body-hugging redingotes' and 'capes from morning to evening – very supple and sometimes double'.

For evening, the designer created 'close-fitting dresses with wide belts, flared sleeves, and lace, organdie or chiffon cuffs', as well as 'dresses of supple velvet, satin, crepe or chiffon with long, flaring corolla-sleeves'.

'At the big, beautiful, inventive Dior show this morning,' *The New York Times* declared, 'Marc Bohan ... made his black dresses and suits look like a million dollars.'

Byzantine Embroidery

Marc Bohan looked to the Orient for his 1968
spring/summer (see right and opposite, top left
and bottom left) and autumn/winter (see opposite,
top right and bottom right) haute couture collections,
with particular nods to the style of the Byzantine
Empire in the 6th century (when Theodora was
its empress), as depicted in the rich mosaics of
the Basilica of San Vitale in Ravenna.

For spring, the designer imagined evening caftans
and dresses, including a 'Theodora robe mantled
in mosaic,' *Vogue* reported. There were also brightly
coloured, flowing gypsy dresses, such as the red
ensemble (right) that was later modelled by Twiggy
and photographed by Richard Avedon for *Vogue*
(which described its 'rush of roses at the wrist
and hem, a clatter of *gitane* gold – the purple
turban sends its streamers flying about the
loose, long gypsy sleeves').

'It's a collection full of honey, flowers and ripples,'
The New York Times declared. 'There are moments
when Marc Bohan, Dior's designer, shows that deep
inside him is a tiny hippie demanding to get out.'

Bohan's autumn/winter collection for the house
(held a few months after the start of the May
1968 events in Paris) featured rich embroideries
in a similar style: tunics, jumpsuits and evening
dresses were adorned with 'bands, and a Byzantine
scroll, in tourmalines, gold beads, silver threads,'
Vogue wrote.

The magazine also focused on the designer's
daywear, praising 'Dior's great pant suits'.
'The proportion's superb,' the magazine proclaimed;
'there isn't a better-looking pants suit in Paris.'

Plastic & Furs

Marc Bohan's spring 1969 collection (see right
and opposite, top left) mixed 'racy day looks –
perfect tailoring and all the snap in the world'
(accessorized with the Dior logo print that
John Galliano would reinterpret over thirty years
later, see p. 316) with 'adorable little Renoir girls'
in white or pastel-coloured dresses, *Vogue* reported.
Cut very short, these delicate silk dresses were
pleated, flounced, or embroidered with white plastic
pieces to create a modern floral motif, as in the
white ensemble pictured opposite (top left).

There are no extant photographs or records
of Bohan's autumn/winter 1969–1970 collection,
but a collection of *'haute fourrure'* was created for
the same season, designed by Frédéric Castet
(see opposite, below left and right). This featured
dramatic furs, from leopard- or zebra-printed
creations (often worn with matching boots and
headpieces), reminiscent of Christian Dior's
own love of animal prints (see, for example,
pp. 24, 33 and 39), to boldly coloured geometric
looks, such as the pink and white beaver coat
shown opposite (bottom left) – 'a madly zippy
short coat playing around with fur as though
it were poster paint,' *Vogue* wrote.

Veils & Paisley

Marc Bohan's spring/summer 1970 collection
(see right and opposite, top left and bottom left)
was particularly praised by the press for its daywear
creations. *Vogue* commented on 'the superb Dior
coats, each more desirable than the other ... belted ...
with a tiny bodice, the sparest neckline closed down
one side'.

'What is memorable at Dior is not only the coats,'
The New York Times added, 'but the cut of the jersey
suits..., the shirts, and the dresses with the assurance
of the crepe de Chine black shirtwaist that is tucked
and pleated only in front.'

Veils and shawls were another highlight of the
collection, with 'Dior's shawled suede' and 'Dior's
marvellous butterscotch suede gaucho culottes
swathed in a big, dashing, tie-silk Paisley shawl
awash with black fringe,' as *Vogue* wrote.

For autumn/winter (see opposite, top right and
bottom right), Bohan presented 'practical, delightful
little jackets, belted pullovers, smashing pants and
skirts to wear under good coats and fur-lined capes
with soft little felt hacking hats and crochet cloches,'
Vogue reported.

The paisley theme of his spring/summer collection
was also revisited in quilted, fur-trimmed satin
evening coats and skirts. 'Any woman anywhere
on earth would want to own these totally feminine
clothes,' *Vogue* proclaimed.

Round Collars
& Cape Sleeves

'Marc Bohan, the Dior designer, was busy
showing the world a spring and summer collection
that more or less updated the American sportswear
look of the 1940s and, for eveningwear, had the
ethereal, romantic look that goes back to the 1930s,'
Bernadine Morris reported for *The New York Times*.

The house's creations that season (see right
and opposite, top left and bottom left) included
broad-shouldered 'clean-cut blazer jackets, swingy
collarless toppers and casual trench coats,' Morris
added, while for evening there were 'filmy dresses
with cape sleeves or cape tops'.

One of the collection's highlights, according
to *Vogue*, was 'the wider-shouldered, big-collared,
big-pocketed, double-breasted bright white
blanket-cloth coat – the one every woman
on earth is going to want to wrap herself
up in' (shown opposite, bottom left).

For his autumn/winter collection (see opposite,
right), Bohan showed 'beautiful clothes that are
often opulent,' *The New York Times* wrote. 'The
effects are achieved through seaming and shaping
in the time-honored couture way. To be specific,
there are charming coats, small through the
bodice and flaring from a high waistline.'

Bohan 'has made a collection that is as deep
and luxurious as sitting in a Maserati with
a splendid fur throw,' *Vogue* added, 'Charming,
unaffected little suits. Wonderful coats ...
big, rounded collars on all.'

Fur & Trouser Suits

'Romance, contemporary-style, is the Parisian
look for spring,' declared *The New York Times*,
which judged Bohan's collection for Dior
(see right) the best of the season in Paris.
'Marc Bohan succeeded in bringing back the
fabled elegance without becoming historical.
There's no pinpointing of the 1930s or 1940s.
The clothes look really contemporary,' wrote
Bernadine Morris. 'They're clothes for women
who are tired of fashion's freaky phase [and]
they include lots of pants with new-looking
flaring or boxy jackets.'

Records of Bohan's autumn/winter 1972–1973
collection have not survived. An *haute fourrure*
collection for the season, designed by Frédéric
Castet (see opposite) made bold use of the
'CD' initials and reinterpreted the elongated
fit of the trouser suits in his spring/summer
collection in zebra- or leopard-patterned fur
versions (one of which, in mink, was modelled
by Pat Cleveland and captured by Irving Penn
in the pages of *Vogue*).

Stripes & Polka Dots

Marc Bohan presented a light and luminous
collection for the spring, dominated by shades
of white and animated by graphic patterns.
Relaxed day suits (with knee-length pleated
skirts) were particularly striking, with their
matching striped or polka-dotted jackets,
skirts, blouses and even hats.

'There is a mood to the collections this spring,
an allure that has to do with the way a modern
woman moves in her clothes and the way clothes
move on a woman,' *Vogue* reported. 'Silhouettes
that flow with the body ... silhouettes that
fit right on the body, small and supple, even
in suits and coats. Nothing is extraneous.
Everything is pared. Simple, very sophisticated
... ultra-feminine.'

'A Bit of Razzle-Dazzle'

'Dior was the one with a bit of razzle-dazzle,'
The New York Times headlined its report on
the Paris couture collections. 'There were
all the neat little touches that mark expensive
clothes, such as blouses printed in the pattern
of the wool tweed of the suits they accompanied,
with a little scarf of the same pattern to tie
around the neck.'

Trouser suits – including bold ensembles in
leather and fur – echoed the elongated line of
the designer's previous collections for the house,
and a new version of the Dior logo print animated
a knee-length fur-trimmed coat (see opposite,
top and right, both designed by Frédéric Castet
for the house's *haute fourrure* collection).

'There were pale crepe de Chine late-day
dresses with the wide, taut midriff that designer
Marc Bohan has been perfecting for a year or so,'
added *The New York Times*. 'They looked so graceful
with their wide skirts nobody even complained
about their longer-than-knee length. And then,
of course, there were the usual dazzling evening
dresses, glowing and glittering with all their might,'
accessorized with feather boas and high-heeled
platform shoes.

Lingerie Dresses
& 'Cigarette' Pyjamas

Marc Bohan infused his spring/summer
collection (see right) with 'the most delicate
feeling of lingerie ever,' *Vogue* wrote, dressing
actress Charlotte Rampling in Dior's silk crepe
georgette creations for its couture report, shot
by Helmut Newton. 'The length doesn't matter,'
Bohan declared, 'it can be short, mid-calf,
or ankle-length, and it will always be pretty.'

For autumn/winter (see opposite), the designer
launched the shorter 'cigarette' pyjama-trousers:
'narrow trousers that stop just above the ankle',
worn with a 'jacket-shirt in lamé or very supple
satin crepe, and sandals,' stated the collection
notes. Ankle length was also adopted in evening
dresses, and there were 'cape-like sleeves that
flutter over the arms' as well as 'two-piece
dresses with long tunic tops that look right
with the longer lengths,' *The New York Times*
reported.

Pointillist Prints
& Hooded Jackets

For spring (see right), 'Marc Bohan does a soft,
very pretty turn on the slim silhouette,' *Vogue*
observed. 'He does pointilliste [*sic*] prints
inspired by the Impressionist painters,' decades
before Raf Simons's 'Pointillist' creations for Dior
(see, for example, pp. 535 and 588–89). 'Colors are
glorious – they glow against the skin. His soft,
printed crêpe de Chine day dresses have bare
necklines – the prettiest, a shallow V so wide
it sometimes slips off the shoulder.'

Reporting on the autumn/winter couture
collections (see opposite), *The New York Times*
declared: 'Mr Bohan's couture styles have an
effortless, uncontrived look. His wrap-around
pleated skirts, which fall gracefully, are a major
contribution to the fall fashion scene.'

'Marc Bohan knows what makes clothes appealing
to women,' *Vogue* echoed in unison, 'the softness
of the fabric, the smallness of the line, the *pretty*
detail. It shows in everything he did – starting
with a group of very good, very luxe coats. Coats
that varied from a hooded, fur-edged raincoat
to a seven-eighths camel coat, to a poncho of
a coat with a hood and plain lining.'

Among *The New York Times*'s highlights were
'a number of silky poplin jackets [with] fur-
trimmed hoods pulled over head-hugging
crocheted caps that in turn cover plain, neat
short hairdos', which it judged particularly
'contemporary'.

'Sportive, Tailored Dressing'

Marc Bohan's spring/summer haute couture
collection for Dior (see right and opposite,
bottom left) focused on masculine-style
tailoring. 'While couture clothes can be heavy,
his are delicate, even his man-tailored suits,'
wrote *The New York Times*.

'The watchword these days is "easy", and Bohan
pursues ease with drawstring. It's a recurrent
theme, from the tailored suits through the chiffon
dresses, and it captures the feeling of softness
that everybody's striving for... Skirts generally
are narrow here for spring, and Bohan manages
to make them practical as well as sexy by
splitting the sides so that women can walk.'

His autumn/winter collection (see opposite,
top left and right) opened with 'sportive, tailored
dressing – trimmed little suits in checks and
stripes ... silk with fur linings, with fur edgings,'
Vogue reported. 'Sports clothes favor knitted
tunics and stove-pipe pants, his mannish suits
have padded shoulders, and harem pants are a
leitmotiv for evening,' *The New York Times* observed.

Bared Shoulders
& White Fox

'Marc Bohan is giving Dior-watchers a lot to
like this season,' *Vogue* reported on this spring/
summer haute couture collection (see right).
'He does it with his bubbly little short dresses.
And he does it by giving shoulders one of the
prettiest hellos in town – bared, framed in
ruffles and sheer pouffy sleeves – and the
throat is wrapped in a wisp of a scarf.'

The designer's autumn/winter collection
(see opposite) proposed a series of equally
glamorous ensembles, including the 'white silk
jacquard pants suit with white fox, white pearls
and bareness underneath – a soft white camisole'
that *Vogue* predicted would be a 'sure-fire'
bestseller that season.

Trouser-suit aficionado Bianca Jagger was in
the audience, and 'said she loved everything –
the capes, the ruffles, the white man-tailored
pants suit,' *The New York Times* stated. 'The music
was 1950s show tunes ("Gigi", "My Fair Lady")
and the styles carried echoes from that time.
Bouffant skirts. Bloused jackets... The fabrics
were revivals too: crisp silk gazar, glittering
metal brocades, puckered matelassés... There
were plenty of prints, including a magnificent
flowered red chiffon.'

Echoes of the 1940s

Vogue praised 'the snap of Dior's racy/jaunty
suiting' in the spring/summer collection (see right),
describing the house's eveningwear as 'a magic
mix of ease/all-out opulence'.

'The news of the season was the return of the
tailored suit,' proclaimed *The New York Times*.
'There were checked pants suits with checked
shirts, narrow ties – and umbrellas used as
walking sticks,' the newspaper reported, while
for evening Bohan proposed 'pale crepe dresses ...
billowing white organdie dresses embellished with
satin ribbon threaded through the waist [and]
white marquisette with red roses embroidered
on the skirt'.

For autumn (see opposite), Bohan 'has gone back
to the pre-Dior years,' *The New York Times* reported.
'Like the rest of the fashion designers here, he's
caught up in what is described as the return of
the 1940s' and the late 1930s of Elsa Schiaparelli.
The main theme of the collection was 'broad
shoulders and a narrow silhouette', often cut
in black satin.

Leather Sashes
& Diamond Skirts

'The star of the Dior runway was the loose jacket, paired either with a skinny skirt or a pair of pants, and which was always shown belted', most often with leather sashes, *The New York Times* reported. Describing Marc Bohan's spring/summer haute couture collection this season (see right and opposite, top left and bottom left), the newspaper added, 'It's worn with ankle-strap sandals, shoulder-length hair and an Art Deco enamel triangle pinned to a beret', while 'stockings have a stripe up the side like the ones on dinner suits'.

Vogue also praised 'a new impact – a line that's broad-shouldered, then narrow, belted from Dior. With the added impact of black and white and a dash of color', featuring Bohan's white belted coat with a black leather sash (opposite, bottom left) in its pages that year.

For autumn, the designer offered up square-shouldered suits with diamond-shaped patterns on skirts for day (such as the satin-trimmed velvet jacket and faille dress shown opposite, bottom right) and satin dresses for evening in bright yellows, greens and oranges (see opposite, top right).

Classicism vs Baroque Fancies

Marc Bohan titled this spring/summer collection
(right) 'Return to Classicism', focusing on a pared-
back silhouette with defined shoulders, supple and
belted waists, and knee-length hemlines. 'My look
is one of softness and neatness. I'm using lots of
blues – from a light navy to a rich greeny-blue,
as well as many blacks and all-whites,' Bohan told
Vogue. Eschewing prints, the designer declared:
'I prefer stripes and I'm using lots of them,
especially wide stripes in two colours.'

'His best design was a jacket with a low double-
breasted closing that worked equally well with
nautical berets for daytime and with embroidered
tops and long skirts for evening,' judged *The
New York Times*. 'His couture spring suits are in
gabardines, flannels, and linens,' *Vogue* reported,
while 'many short crêpe evening dresses have
one-shouldered necklines'.

For autumn/winter (see opposite), Bohan was
inspired by 'Baroque fancies and pre-Raphaelite
chinoiserie,' the collection notes read. Echoing the
dramatic sashes of his spring/summer collection
the previous year (see pp. 188–89), the designer
created 'sinuous and supple bias-cut evening
dresses pleated "à la Fortuny" decorated with
inlays, tulle or lace,' the house stated.

'Easy, Flowing Styles'

For his spring/summer haute couture collection
(see right), Marc Bohan 'stayed with easy, flowing
styles that were the most contemporary,' *The New
York Times* proclaimed. Presented at the Hotel
de Crillon (the show having been moved from
the traditional avenue Montaigne salons due
to the number of guests expected), the collection
included 'the basic suit [with] ankle-length,
wide-ish trousers, sometimes cuffed', while
'dresses developed the drawstring theme
Bohan has been playing with for years'.

'The drawstrings appear at the waistline and
a few inches up from the hem' and 'the dresses
often have short puffed sleeves and are scattered
with cheerful motifs like red dots,' the newspaper
added. 'Bohan has created styles that not only
uphold the honor of the couture but can be worn
comfortably as well.'

For autumn/winter, the designer offered up
checked suits with sweeping ankle-length skirts,
accessorized with scarves. 'The looser clothes were
cinched in at the waist with corselet-type belts',
while 'at night, black with gold was the prevailing
theme and there were wonderful effects of gold
lamé, gold brocade and black velvet [see opposite],'
The New York Times reported.

Graphic Patterns
& Aubrey Beardsley

Marc Bohan's spring collection for Dior (see right and opposite, left) focused on bright colours and striking graphic motifs, from stripes to polka dots. The silhouette was relaxed and ethereal, with plays on transparency. *Vogue* reported on 'Marc Bohan's strong graphic patterns, black-and-white' and dressed actress Isabella Rossellini in Dior's 'unexpected Pierrot "pyjama" ... and on-the-bias silk satin crêpe dress in panels, over narrowing pants ... a great mix of polka dots' in its spring couture report.

Bohan's autumn/winter collection (see opposite, right) paid homage to 'Aubrey Beardsley and his wild drawings in the late Victorian age,' *The New York Times* wrote. 'Turbans and feather headdresses, lace pantalettes and sweetheart necklines are some of the mad paraphernalia recaptured from the 19th century'.

Trompe L'œil
& Sinuous Dresses

The theme of Dior's spring/summer couture collection (see right) was trompe l'œil. There were trompe l'œil belts and lapels on 'triangular' suits (with wide shoulders and cinched waists), accessorized with sailor hats and two-tone berets. Trompe l'œil motifs were also printed on dresses. Eveningwear featured cocoon dresses in gazar. The collection was widely praised and won Bohan his first Golden Thimble award.

'Sporty, sophisticated, sinuous, supple, sexy' – this is how the show notes introduced Bohan's autumn/winter collection (see opposite). Shoulders were enlarged, the waist lowered, and suits had a 'masculine-feminine' edge. For evening, there were 'scarf dresses', 'military dresses', 'kilt dresses' and 'sinuous' dresses with long 'mermaid' skirts.

Klimt vs Pollock

Praised by *Women's Wear Daily* as 'a beautifully
tailored, flattering and feminine collection',
Marc Bohan's spring/summer haute couture
presentation (see right) focused on a long
silhouette, 'built in supple gabardine or wool
suits, or belted silk dresses' with 'long and loose'
jackets. The designer's most striking creations,
however, were a series of garments decorated
with 'Klimt embroidery' (many years before
Galliano's own Klimt-inspired designs; see p. 456):
'long tunics, camisoles, jackets or gowns, entirely
embroidered in gold on white, white tone-on-tone,
or in vivid hues of violet, fuchsia, turquoise-blue
and yellow,' read the collection notes.

For autumn/winter (see opposite), Bohan
placed his collection 'under the sign of opposites,'
explained the collection notes. There were
'tight dresses and oversized coats and jackets,
tweed and diamonds, bright colours on a black
background'. After Gustav Klimt the previous
season, Bohan looked to the work of Abstract
Expressionist painter Jackson Pollock to create
bright 'drip' embroidery and print motifs,
which adorned short evening bolero jackets
and floor-length sheath dresses (sometimes
accessorized with 'Pollock' jewels in jet and
multicoloured stones).

Zig-Zag Dresses
& Sharp Suits

'Wide shoulders, slim waist, long legs' read the
title of the collection notes for this spring/summer
haute couture collection (see right). Decades after
Christian Dior's original 'Zig-Zag' line (see p. 30),
there were 'asymmetrical "zig-zag"' evening
dresses, as well as draped or 'red-lacquer'
embroidered sheath dresses with 'obi' belts,
the house explained.

For his autumn/winter haute couture collection
(see opposite), Marc Bohan produced sharp suits
with tightly cinched waists summoning the spirit
of the original 1947 'Bar' jacket, accessorized
with 'constellations-themed' jewels.

Women's Wear Daily noted the 'young at heart'
feel of 'his naughty, smart-chic collection for
Dior'. 'Hips are wrapped for attention, the knee
is revealed,' the magazine reported. 'The new
silhouette, always cut to flirtatious advantage,
outlines bosoms with bustier tops, sometimes
appliqued onto simple turtleneck dresses.'

Peplum Waists

Marc Bohan concentrated on black and white
contrasts in his spring/summer haute couture
collection (see right), which *Women's Wear Daily*
described as 'unsparingly spare with a simplicity
that gave them the neuter sleekness of Concorde
uniforms'. There was no 'chi-chi', the designer
declared.

But if colours were kept relatively simple, shapes
were particularly strong. 'A new soft peplumed
waist – in a Dior suit' caught *Vogue*'s attention.
'The waist provides his liveliest contour, nipped
and curved in the cleaned-up redingotes and
peplum jackets he has adapted from his couture,
for last fall [see p. 201], or underlined with big
black patent leather belts, the key accessory,'
Women's Wear Daily reported.

For autumn/winter (see opposite), Bohan
produced a collection that 'dared to get into
the new eccentric mood,' *Women's Wear Daily*
declared. There were whimsical jewels (from
'arrow' earrings to heart-shaped Dior brooches)
and dramatic peplum shapes carried over from
his previous haute couture collection.

Women's Wear Daily also noted 'hip-accenting
pockets and short lean skirts; sparkle for day,
in the metallic-flecked jersey dress; ... burlesque
cock-feather-trim pockets on suits and wild
evening dresses with billowy taffeta skirts
opening over short, lean, beaded skirts'.

The New Look Turns 40

Marking the 40th anniversary of the house's
creation and titled 'Dior Toujours', Marc Bohan's
1987 spring/summer haute couture collection
(see right) reworked Dior's famous tailoring,
with 'rounded shoulders, square shoulders [and]
patent belts' for day, the collection notes stated.
For evening, the designer presented a series of
short, flouncy 'Belle Epoque' dresses decorated
with taffeta or gazar, as well as majestic long
'corolla' and 'fan' dresses.

The following season (see opposite), the essence
of the designer's line was described in the collection
notes as 'round shoulders, high waist, short skirts'.
There were high-waisted coat-dresses cut in
traditionally 'masculine' fabrics, square necklines,
fur trims and flared 'can-can' dresses.

'The new New Look was celebrated ... with the
same extravagant use of fabric in big coats cut
wide and swinging over the new short, short skirt,'
The Times reported. 'To emphasize the flirty new
hemlines, Marc Bohan whips them around with
mink and chinchilla, or stiffens them with wire
to stand out like a bell.'

Micro-Hats
& Masquerades

Marc Bohan's spring/summer haute couture
collection (see right) presented 'some of the best
suits money can buy,' *Women's Wear Daily* declared.
Day ensembles included 'suits, dresses and redingotes
with "corselet" waists,' the house explained, as well
as '"lingerie" blouses and dresses with corselet busts,
trimmed with print or dotted mousseline ruffles'.
For evening, there were short 'off-the-shoulder
décolleté' dresses with 'three-quarter sleeves' and
'"scarf-dresses" in zebra puckered gauze' or 'with
"sarong" wrapping, draped with an asymmetrical
décolleté ending in a scarf'.

Bohan's autumn/winter collection (see opposite)
– awarded the Golden Thimble prize for best haute
couture collection that season – was both luxurious
(with gold brocades, fur trims and rich embroideries)
and whimsical (with dramatic, feather-like volumes
and a masquerade theme complete with black
velvet masks both real and embroidered over
short evening jackets).

'The Indian Year'

Baptized 'The Indian Year', Marc Bohan's last
haute couture collection for Dior chose the colours,
spirit and traditional dress of India as its theme
(as Gianfranco Ferré would for his final haute
couture collection for the house, too; see p. 254).

Mixing the pink, yellow and orange tones emblematic
of Indian dress with Christian Dior's favoured floral
motifs (embroidered or printed), Bohan proposed
'Pyramid and Sari lines', with long saris in gazar
or silk chiffon for evening and 'pyramid' coats in
pastel suede for day.

Suits weren't forgotten, however: there were
'short or long flared jackets [with] small shoulders,
shirt collars' and 'flared jackets in embroidered
suede with "flower pot" and "window-box" themes
[worn] over short or long pleated culotte-skirts
in silk chiffon'.

'The couture ladies made a beeline to Dior the
day after the show for Marc Bohan's safely chic
suits and irresistibly simple chiffons,' *Women's
Wear Daily* reported.

Gianfranco Ferré

Coding Dior

The appointment of Gianfranco Ferré to Christian Dior in May 1989 was an event. Firstly, it was a coup – Ferré was one of the most fashionable and acclaimed designers of the period, and the first to be appointed by Bernard Arnault, the 40-year-old French financial wizard who had purchased Dior as part of a nearly bankrupt company named Agache-Willot-Boussac in 1984, nursing it back to robust financial health and Dior back to international prominence. But there was more: in the house's 32 years of existence, Ferré was only the fourth artistic director, to use a modern turn-of-phrase never uttered by Monsieur Dior (who referred to himself only as a 'couturier'). Ferré was also the first that hadn't known Dior personally – indeed, both Yves Saint Laurent and Marc Bohan had been employed by Dior himself.

Yet, despite his talent being born from the ready-to-wear industry of Milan, rather than the rarefied haute couture ateliers of Paris, Ferré perhaps had more in common with Dior than either of his predecessors. Their physical resemblance was striking, albeit with the addition of a beard in Ferré's case; Dior was 41 when he founded his *maison*, Ferré 45 when he took over the reins; both were emotionally bound to their mothers – Dior reviving the Belle Époque heyday of his, and Ferré returning often to sleep at his mother's home, even in the midst of his Dior success. And while Dior's fashion was less radical than Saint Laurent's, and more romantic than Bohan's, in Ferré he would have found an ideal aesthetic counterpart, one who appreciated Dior's love of decoration, stylized silhouettes, glamour and adoration of unabashed femininity. Ferré had experimented with similar styles under his own label in the eighties, producing grand evening dresses and curvaceous daywear with a Dolce Vita fifties hint that, in retrospect, bore a whispered signature. It was easy to get from Dolce Vita to Dior.

However, despite their aesthetic similarities, Ferré's appointment to Dior was an acknowledgment of a shift in the fashion industry: from haute couture as a necessity for women, albeit women who could afford to spend tens of thousands on single outfits, to haute couture as a necessity for business.

Haute couture had become a valuable marketing tool. By the late eighties, there was a bubbling mood of change at Dior – a need not just for evolution, but for revolution.

Originally trained as an architect at the Politecnico di Milano, Ferré established his own ready-to-wear business in Milan in 1978, during a boom time of Italian fashion. Drawing attention through womenswear that revelled in intricate construction and dramatic silhouette – both signatures of Dior – Ferré was dubbed 'the architect of fashion' (his actual title, after that architecture degree, was *Il Dottore Architetto*), and his collections revived the complex structures and overscale proportions that had lent such impact to Dior's debut in 1947. If Dior built dresses, so did Ferré.

Ferré took Dior's New Look as his lynchpin throughout his seven-year tenure, creating a curvaceous silhouette emphasized by outsize elements – lapels, cuffs, tightly cinched belts. He combined houndstooth checks with lace, tucked flowers inside the necklines of vast ball gowns, and launched the Lady Dior handbag. This was quilted with a 'cannage' pattern lifted from the cane-backed chairs Dior favoured in his salons – just as those flowers, those ball gowns, that mix of lace and wool, that fusion of masculine and feminine, were also cleverly drawn from Dior's past. Ferré was the first to use Dior's history as the foundation, as the cornerstone, of its new look for the eighties and nineties. 'I don't want to live with a ghost,' he declared. 'But I respect the couture tradition.'

What Ferré did at Dior wasn't limited to clothes. In essence, his remit was not to reinvent Dior, but to revive it, to establish house codes that could represent Dior in a new era – codes that could translate from the heights of haute couture, through ready-to-wear, to perfumes, accessories and beauty. Not a new look, but a new identity – using the elements of the past to create the future.

Alexander Fury

'Ascot – Cecil Beaton'

Created to evoke the 'freedom of a masculine-feminine charm', 'Ascot – Cecil Beaton' was Gianfranco Ferré's first haute couture collection for Dior.

Inspired by the Edwardian high-society style of the costumes Cecil Beaton created for the 1964 film *My Fair Lady* (directed by George Cukor), the collection paid particular homage to the film's central scene, set at Royal Ascot, in which men in sharply tailored grey tails and matching top hats mix with women in white floor-length lace dresses trimmed with black bows and ribbons to watch the horse races.

For day, Ferré chose to contrast 'austere masculine fabrics – tweed, barathea, flannel, Prince of Wales check – with exquisitely feminine white blouses in silk, voile and organza' and to play with 'the fluid charm of kimono sleeves', all in a palette of grey, black, white and beige.

For evening, the designer presented an abundance of floor-length dresses in silk faille, duchesse satin, taffeta and shimmering organza, embroidered with interlacing pearls and gems, flecked with gold and silver, or adorned with cascades of flowers – roses, lilies of the valley, country garden flowers and ivy – in turn pinned, printed or embroidered.

A triumphant Dior debut for Gianfranco Ferré, the collection was awarded the prestigious Golden Thimble prize the same year.

'A Midsummer Night's Dream'

Gianfranco Ferré's second haute couture collection
for Dior was 'all about lightness,' the show notes
stated. Divided into five acts ('Suddenly, Last
Summer', 'Parades, Cities and Parks', 'Flowers in
the Garden', 'Gems, Dreams and Mysteries' and,
finally, 'Nights, Places and Palaces') and named
after William Shakespeare's comedy, the collection
set out to evoke 'early dusk in summertime'.

'A breeze caresses the organza, shimmering and
feather-light. Summer is here, dazzling and colourful
in mauve, lilac, dark green, ochre, grey, white, saffron
yellow,' read the collection notes. 'The exquisite sheen
of straw in silk satin. Fabrics such as never before ...
layerings of lace, embroideries, transparent effects
and *trompe l'œil*. And all as light as summer air.'

There was 'a hint of wit and humour as well with
a contrast of opposites such as an organza raincoat,
knotted at the waist with a big bow and worn with
a huge straw hat' (see opposite, bottom right).

The designer 'remains attached to his idea of clothes
that move with the body,' the house declared. 'He
favours body-skimming shapes with very straight
trousers or skirts, puff-sleeved jackets or ribbon-tied
waists in reversible tulle.'

Hats are dramatic, with '*capelines* [wide-brimmed
hats] gently shading the face', and 'his laces, lilacs,
piqués, shantungs, his striped silks, taffetas and
draped effects all constantly enhance a woman's
every movement, while his layering of fabrics gives
volume – in readiness for dreams on a midsummer's
night'.

'Fables and Tales on a Winter's Night'

After his Shakespearean 'Midsummer Night's Dream' the previous season (see p. 216), Gianfranco Ferré baptized his new haute couture presentation for the house 'Fables and Tales on a Winter's Night'.

He 'captured the starry nights of the Orient and all the magic of their myths and fables with deep blues, violets, indigos and shades of ink, with pale pink moons and silvery stars,' stated the collection notes.

'Imperial nights in a never-ending dream of taffeta, ottoman, velvet, silk and duchesse satin. Melting into dusky pinks – magenta, tea rose and Indian rose or flaring into reds, purples, glistening golds and the rich gem-like shades of garnet. Colours that enhance an appealing trompe l'œil of fruit and flowers, a carpet print, reminiscent of the mysterious East or gleaming silver-thread-embroidered brooches. Sumptuous gold and ruby embroideries sparkle with a thousand and one lights on the lapel of a jacket.'

'The mood is completely soft with lots of draping Dior style: couture drapes,' Ferré told *Women's Wear Daily*. 'The silhouette is close to the body but not restricting – it floats.' 'There's a touch of Tiepolo,' the designer added. 'It all starts from the idea of making the face softer with turban-like fabrics, but more natural than turbans.'

'Rendez-Vous d'Amour'

Gianfranco Ferré embraced a light and romantic mood for this collection, baptized 'Rendez-Vous d'Amour' (Love rendez-vous) and split into five evocatively titled acts ('Love letter', 'Fondest memory', 'Spring is here!', 'High summer' and 'Sleepless nights').

'Tomorrow is springtime, when fresh new colours burst into shimmering bouquets,' read the collection notes. 'Fairy-tale shades of pink fuchsia, coral, orange and tender blue; the pale blue of a spring sky, the deep blue of a summer night.'

'Under the pergolas women swirl and rustle in their asymmetrical dresses. The silhouette is pure and essential. The fabrics are opulent and supple, airily contrasting matt and shiny materials crafted into fitted wild silk coat-dresses, gabardine suits and white gazar coats.'

Setting out to illustrate 'opulence in lightness', Ferré sought to 'update the great Dior classics, such as those huge organza bows [see overleaf] or a witty celebration of dogstooth, glen plaid, feathers... Black, white but also wide pink stripes,' the house stated.

'I wanted to lighten up the fantasy,' the designer told *Vogue*. 'I always think of a woman moving in or against a breeze. There's a sense of air within the folds of a fabric, or in stoles or trains, even in a full ball dress.'

'I am mad for bows and big hats,' Ferré added, 'because they give effect, balance and fresh detail. A hat is a flirt – a face-framing disguise to appear or disappear under. Women love dramatic accessories.'

'Autumn Splendour'

Baptized 'Autumn Splendour' ('Soleils d'automne'
in French), this haute couture collection unfolded
in the season's tones of red, gold, black and beige,
rendered in suitably luxurious fabrics and with
an emphasis on drapes, scarves, stoles and pleats.

'It's one of those mild autumn days when mellow
sunlight filters through those last abandoned leaves,'
read the collection notes. This season, the Dior
woman 'is wearing a soft, geometrical suit, which
she has accessorised with a shawl thrown over her
shoulders... Her silhouette gracefully sways in the
lithe, elegant and airy-light line of a silk moiré
"chenille" suit or a cashmere coat.'

'On another day, she is dressed in a salt-and-pepper
woollen suit. Gradually she unfolds what she has
been hiding, playing with materials – camel hair,
taffeta, silk, fur, damask, cashmere, silk crepe,
tweed or dogstooth, and having fun with tortoise-
shell-look sequins, crocodile-look quilted silk or
even [a] python or lizard skirt. She loves the sandy
shades but this time is going for a stroll in reds and
pinks as bright and as glowing as Chinese lacquer.'

Finally, 'when night falls, redolent with the
fragrances of evening celebrations, she envelops
herself in gold to dance under the splendid stucco
of ancient palaces', with creations as glamorous as
the gleaming silver evening gown worn by Karen
Mulder for the collection's finale (see overleaf,
bottom left).

'In Balmy Summer Breezes'

Gianfranco Ferré takes us into Christian Dior's
beloved gardens with this nature-inspired
collection entitled 'In Balmy Summer Breezes'.

'On splendid summer mornings when the
heat begins to rise over sun-soaked parks and
gardens, softly imbued with a hazy and sensuous
atmosphere, now is the time for lazy strolls,
chance encounters and midnight parties – a
time when light, vaporous silhouettes rustle along
the pathways and silk organza, taffeta and gazar
flutter in the balmy summer breezes,' read the
collection notes.

'Sun-bright flowers, touches of lace, sun-yellow
straw, grassy greens and heavenly blues' gave the
collection its bright colours and inspired striking
wide-brimmed straw hats for couture gardeners.

Ferré's garden also counted 'elegant women
dressed in loose embroidered flower-printed gazar
shirts, giant red and black gingham suits, gleaming
tartans, contrasts of stripes and houndstooth, tulle
and embroidered white cotton fishnet skirts with
basques, silk herringbone pants-suits, long ruffled
tulle and satin ribbon fishnet dresses and sunny
yellow taffeta over-jackets'.

Before a finale of spectacular floral evening
gowns, the designer stopped 'under the pergola'
with trompe l'œil silk dresses embroidered by
Lesage to evoke 'glistening columns overgrown
with acanthus leaves' (see p. 233, bottom right).

'In the Secret of a Venetian Winter'

Gianfranco Ferré looked to his native Italy
for inspiration for this haute couture collection.
Dominated by red, gold and grey tones and titled
'In the Secret of a Venetian Winter', it reflected
not only the trademark colours of the city, but
also its 18th-century splendour.

This season, the Dior woman 'loves wearing these
mid-length charcoal grey dresses that she brightens
with a silver fox bolero – in fact, she simply adores
all the greys: those flight-delaying foggy greys,
elephant grey or the grey marble of Venetian
palaces, soft greying shadows over Venice... Grey
shadows lit by the fire and flames of tone-on-tone
reds,' proclaimed the collection notes.

'She loves to wear a black, grey or white coat
or suit enhanced with a touch of red brought
by a hat, a blouse or even a flower, but this
is not enough for her: she also feels she needs
mineral colours glowing like precious gems –
a double-faced ruby red and amethyst coat,
a ruby satin embroidered scarf, a trompe l'œil
dress with lapis lazuli overstitching effect.'

'She wears dove-coloured woollen suits with beige
chinchilla cuffs or a red ottoman wool coat with
gold-trimmed overstitched red-leather facing.
And she just adores spectacular details, like big
coat collars, elaborate black leather cuffs or velvet
necklaces... She dreams about the allegories of
the 18th-century Venetian galas – the beauty
of the amber shades of marble, the muted gold
of frescoes.'

'Summer Impressions'

Staying in the 18th century after his Venice-
inspired autumn/winter haute couture collection
dedicated to the reds and golds of La Serenissima
(see p. 234), Gianfranco Ferré looked to the work
of 18th-century French Rococo painter Jean-Honoré
Fragonard and Italian neoclassical sculptor Antonio
Canova, famous for his white marble sculptures
(the colour that took centre stage in this collection).

Setting the scene for a summer sunrise where
'long, slender silhouettes begin to appear in an
almost diaphanous whiteness: a sublime aura of
white that intermingles with neo-classic dreams,
haunted by Antonio Canova and Fragonard,'
the collection notes described 'an impression
of lightness, of fluidity, of freedom: all those
impalpable summer impressions'.

'In shell-pleats, puff sleeves, flared hems, these
feminine apparitions gracefully glide to the
movement of their soft, loose, light-as-air clothes.
A wayward wind wafts through great clouds
of shot taffeta – all the delights of transparent
organza, worn next to the skin… The rediscovered
joys of long, draped effects, of pleated suits or
perhaps low-necked shirt dresses. Then the suave
intoxication of transparent black macramé and
brown straw-lace sculpted like primitive attire.'

'Images in a Mirror'

Dedicated to the splendours of the Renaissance,
Gianfranco Ferré's haute couture collection was
baptized 'Images in a Mirror', the better to celebrate
haute couture as essentially 'extra-ordinary'.

'Haute Couture is not an answer to everyday
dressing but the echo of our dreams and our
intuitive, out-of-the-ordinary visions,' Ferré wrote
by way of introduction to the collection. 'It is a
way of discovering new sensations, new feelings
that intermingle with new and sensually rich
shapes.'

'For this 1993–94 Fall-Winter Collection, I wanted
something more shapely, more supple with a freer
and more vibrant allure ... [rediscovering] the
amazing chromatic alchemy of Titian – the depth
and intensity of his reds, his purples, golds and
midnight blues. The delightful nuances of Veronese
that voluptuously dissolve into the lovely colourful
saturation of his inimitable browns, reds and greens.'

'We can feel a hidden passion under these shades
of painted or traditionally hand-woven brocades
– wonderful fabrics such as a golden cascade of
crushed silk, printed cashmeres, suede trimmed
and incrusted herringbone... Long dresses whose
vertical lines flap like banners in the breeze.'

'Summer Paradox'

Gianfranco Ferré summoned the spirit of 'French
eccentricity' for this collection (baptized 'Summer
Paradox'), and more particularly the style of the
'Merveilleuses' (who favoured revealing light white
tunics inspired by Ancient Greece and Rome) and
the 'Incroyables' in the aftermath of the French
Revolution in the late 18th century (who would
also, coincidentally, be one of John Galliano's key
references). Ferré also took inspiration from the
city of Naples and all its treasures.

'An intensely blue sky – strong shades combined
with the softness of straw – hidden flowers, floral
petticoats,' read the collection notes. The silhouette
was very feminine, with 'rounded bodices, flared
skirts, puffed sleeves'. There were also trompe l'œil
effects with 'skirts flat in the front with exaggerated
behinds, and jackets short in the front and long
at the back'.

The designer's colour palette was discreet and
delicate with coral, pink, yellow, turquoise, porcelain
and Wedgwood-blue tones and paisley prints, while
fabrics were kept as light as possible and ranged
from cashmere and chiffon to raffia, linen, wild silk,
silk jacquard and towelling.

'Winter in an Extraordinary Forest'

The mood for this collection, entitled 'Winter in an Extraordinary Forest', sought to evoke 'fantasmagorical dream visions of a magical nature, metamorphosed by alchemy and passion,' according to the collection notes.

'Unexpected touches of colour, almost invisible to the human eye, snap the natural balance. The memory of imaginary insects, enchanted leaves and fabulous animals reinvent the Mystery-Woman,' the house stated.

The silhouette, 'as blurred as some wintry apparition', was characterized by 'round cuts for flowing, rounded lines' and 'a new fullness for the shoulders and bust, emphasized by a more defined and curvy waistline'.

Flower effects were obtained 'by lacquered crushing', while 'the most supple laces in the world [were] metamorphosed into magical carpets of leaves' and accessories included 'bark-jewellery or brilliant dragonfly jewels' for a sylvan touch in line with the collection's theme.

'Extreme'

Gianfranco Ferré looked to 20th-century art
to inspire the collection he baptized 'Extreme' –
more specifically, to the styles of Nicolas de Staël,
Andy Warhol and Jackson Pollock for 'a journey
into irrational colour'.

As the collection notes stated, the designer set
out to create 'a palimpsest of different eras, skillful
layerings of many centuries and influences: haute
couture is upsetting conformity and has fun with
tradition'.

The overall silhouette flirted with 'the 1950s look'.
'Organza rounds out the hips, creating an extremely
shapely figure that plays on femininity. The bust
is on view, while the shoulders are narrow but
well constructed. The waist is always defined,
often nipped in, sometimes even strangled.'

Organza was the star fabric for this collection,
accompanied by 'candy-yellow silk, buttercup lace,
and sunny shades of tulle – colour forms the link
from one material to another'.

'Tribute to Paul Cézanne'

This collection paid tribute to painter Paul Cézanne, ahead of the retrospective of the artist's work that would shortly be shown at Paris's Grand Palais.

'Christian Dior dedicated collections to Vermeer and to Watteau,' the house stated. 'The tribute to a great painter is therefore a tribute to Christian Dior himself and to his way of finding inspiration.'

'Gianfranco Ferré is offering Cézanne and Dior a firework display of free creativity, in a subtle choreography drawn from Cézanne's own colours and tonalities. Light and intensely rhythmic movement filled with warm affection for the classic genius of modern painting,' read the collection notes, which likened Cézanne to the 'couturier' of an 'exclusive client': the Sainte-Victoire mountain in Aix-en-Provence.

'To pay tribute to Cézanne, Dior has borrowed from the magical tonalities of the painter's work. Shadows brightened by touches of light, sombre colours sparked by some shining star, like a "little bit of sunshine on cold water", from the palette of his early years', with shades of greys, blacks and browns highlighted here and there with touches of red from *Afternoon in Naples*, cobalt from *Blue Vase*, vermilion from *Plate of Apples*, or emerald green from *Mont Sainte-Victoire*.

The line itself combined 'very fitted cuts, preserving ease and comfort, with an elegant allure ... a subtle harmony of rounded shoulders and curvy hips that emphasizes and enhances femininity without hindering it'.

'In Christian Dior's Garden'

Gianfranco Ferré turned to one of the house's founder's great passions with this collection baptized 'In Christian Dior's Garden'.

Monsieur Dior was even quoted at the head of the collection notes: 'I designed clothes for flower-like women with soft shoulders, blossoming busts, lithe, slender waists and skirts as full as corollas... Flowers, after women, are the finest gift God has given to the world,' the couturier had written.

With this collection, Ferré set out to evoke 'all the mystery of flower-women. Springtime buds barely burst open. A hint of pink, vanilla, almond or early-morning mist. Laces tucked away under boyish suits. Brazen petticoats blending the fiery summer lights of sumptuous summer dresses into stormy skies.'

There were two key silhouettes: 'one is body-skimming, underlining the bust, cinching the waist, rounding the shoulders and shaping the hips. The other is swirling, romantic, petticoated, and plays with trains, pleated organza and embroidered laces,' the house stated.

'Darts, piping, stitching and bias cuts' served to 'highlight the fullness of the skirts', while natural silk reigned 'in all its forms: shantung, taffeta, organdie, organza, chiffon, faille, satin and twill'.

Colours were the central element of this collection, each introduced in the collection notes by quotations chosen from *Christian Dior's Little Dictionary of Fashion*. Grey was 'the most convenient, useful and elegant neutral colour', while white 'is the most beautiful colour that exists for the evening', but pink and its many shades dominated the collection: 'the softest colour of all,' according to Christian Dior. 'Every woman should have something pink in her wardrobe. It's the colour of happiness and femininity.'

'Indian Passion'

Gianfranco Ferré's final haute couture collection
for Dior, titled 'Indian Passion', was inspired by the
treasures and colours of India, to which the designer
made many extended trips in the 1970s.

Described by the house as 'an odyssey of colours',
it looked both to the West, 'where the classic
black and white geometrical designs, traditional
to Christian Dior, are being highlighted ... accented
here and there with subtle touches of animal prints',
and to 'a contemporary passion for an imaginary
East' with 'a burst of bright satin ... quilted
overstitched cashmere, taffeta or silk overjackets'.

The dominant colours for the collection reflected
its central theme, with 'glimmering Bengal lights,
glowing ember, purple or violet reds' and of course
graduated shades of pink (famously described by
Diana Vreeland as 'the navy blue of India'), as well
as fawn and copper tones 'with some gold and
amber to enhance every gesture and complete this
sumptuous rainbow, only composed of the warmest
tones'.

The silhouette was 'soft and straight'. 'Dresses
are regal-looking, tunic styles, modest and
flowing. Daytime is dominated by strict and simple
Cartesian cuts and the eternal elegance of masculine
fabrics... For the evening, dresses are longer and
fuller. The dinner dress or the gala gown, the
sheath dress or the silk, chiffon or organza crinoline,
all take flight in a sensuous swirl of arabesque
embroidered laces, sequins and pearls. Nothing
is too sumptuous for them.'

John Galliano

The Revolution, Anew

How to mark the fiftieth anniversary of Christian Dior's revolutionary
New Look? With another revolution. In 1996, the British designer
John Galliano – a plumber's son, born in Gibraltar in 1960 but raised in
London – became the creative director of the esteemed and august house
of Christian Dior. His first creation was for Diana, Princess of Wales, to wear
to a gala at New York's Metropolitan Museum of Art, opening an exhibition
to celebrate Dior's work. Staged in December 1996, that exhibition (and
dress) coincided – to the month – with the fiftieth anniversary of the house's
founding. John Galliano's first haute couture collection, in January 1997,
was a historical landmark before it was even presented.

Galliano's ascent to Dior was as perfectly fitting as one of his couture suits.
He had been enamoured with the work of Dior for years, staging shows in Paris
that paid homage to that past master's silhouettes, his techniques, and most of
all his unabashed embrace of voluptuous femininity. His shows, simultaneously,
were a curriculum vitae, a clarion call as to Galliano's eminent suitability for
the conferral of one of fashion's greatest honours and foremost responsibilities.
Galliano himself described the preceding five years as a rehearsal for his role.
'It's the greatest house in the world,' he stated, visibly cowed, in a British
documentary filmed at the end of 1996. 'To be given the reins of the house
is something I would never have believed could happen. How could I say no?'

How could the house of Dior say no, either, given that Galliano's arch
romanticism and mastery of cut made him seem like the founder's contemporary
incarnation? Galliano's skill was evident from his first collection: his 1984
Saint Martin's BA graduation collection, titled 'Les Incroyables' after a band
of eighteenth-century dandies, caused a sensation and launched his career
internationally. Galliano's clothes ever since had been heaped with laurels –
not least after his appointment to the house of Givenchy (owned, like Dior,
by French businessman Bernard Arnault), which made Galliano the first
British designer to helm a French haute couture house since World War II.
It was a stunning endorsement.

Galliano's debut was eagerly anticipated, and hyperbolically reviewed.
'Mr. Galliano's show was a credit to himself, to Mr. Dior, whose name is

on the door, and to the future of the art, which is always in question,' wrote Amy Spindler in *The New York Times*, of that spring/summer 1997 haute couture show. But it was true of his tenure as a whole: Galliano's vision for Dior was vast – multi-faceted, complex, looking simultaneously backwards and forwards. He turned Dior inside out and upside down – literally, in terms of collections that deconstructed the house's haute couture traditions, pushing forward to find something brave and new.

Galliano looked far beyond the New Look. He was determined to create new looks of his own, new hallmarks for the house of Dior in the twenty-first century. Yet, even through his constant revolutions, there was always a respect and reverence for the past. Even a show devoted to sexual fetishism was rooted in silhouettes drawn from the Dior archives – but Galliano's creativity was inflamed by a need not to rehash, but to re-imagine what Dior could represent to modern women.

Galliano's goal at Dior – achieved with spectacular success – was to take a historical template and not just work within its confines, but redefine them. Those confines were not limited to the instantly identifiable New Look, but to the whole of Dior itself. Galliano thumbed his nose at the bourgeois foundations of both haute couture and the house of Dior – the first creative director since Yves Saint Laurent to do so. This approach resulted in a strikingly modern, re-energized vision of Dior, returning the house to the pinnacle of influence in the fashion industry and redefining how – and how much – a creative director could re-invent the image of a label. Galliano's revitalization of Dior proved a creative and commercial success, a template others would follow.

Galliano's tenure at Christian Dior has been perhaps irrevocably sullied by his personal demons – he was dismissed in March 2011, following a drunken tirade of racist and anti-Semitic abuse at a Parisian bar (he has since been rehabilitated). But his legacy is indelible. He created fashion that served not only as a testament to Christian Dior's lasting genius, but also as a stunning demonstration of his own.

Alexander Fury

Maasai Mitzah

Marking the fiftieth anniversary of the house, John Galliano's first collection for Dior was staged at the Grand Hotel in Paris, where a scaled-up version of Dior's original haute couture salons had been built, complete with majestic staircase, gold chairs and Dior-grey hangings.

'I wanted to get behind Monsieur Dior and what was inspiring him,' Galliano told Colin McDowell. 'Mitzah Bricard, the pearls, the perfume his mother wore, the whole Belle Epoque silhouette of his mother that he was obsessed with, and then draw parallels with the Maasai tribe, with these two fantastic silhouettes – which are incredibly similar, proud, aristocratic: that was my starting-off point.'

Triggered by Galliano's discovery of Mirella Ricciardi's famous photographs of the African tribe, the Maasai inspiration was intertwined with the tightly corseted 'S-line' silhouette and moulded mermaid dresses captured by painter Giovanni Boldini in his portraits of Edwardian beauties.

Dior's iconic 'Bar'-line (see p. 24) was revisited, 'dramatically shortened and deliberately softened' in '*masculin-féminin* dandy fabrics like houndstooth or Prince of Wales' or embroidered white leather cut to evoke lace, in creations such as 'Diorbella' (p. 262, right) or 'Gallidior' (p. 262, left).

Mitzah Bricard, Christian Dior's muse, inspired both a shade of lilac that Galliano baptized 'Mitzah's lilac' and used in all of the satin linings, and the presence of feline leopard print (one of the hallmarks of her style), which appeared on 'lingerie dresses ... and on painted hair saucers, to give a humorously chic and sophisticated touch to hairstyles'.

The Maasai brought 'their multicolor ornaments, breastplates, tiny pearled corsets, plate-collars and multiple bracelets to brighten the allure while instilling the body with a noble and proud bearing', while 'travel-associated exoticism ... is also inspired by a European infatuation for Chinese taste and *chinoiserie*'.

A motif that would come to the fore in Galliano's following collection for the house (see p. 266), *chinoiserie* was here most evident in 'Absinthe' (right), the chartreuse-coloured satin sheath dress inspired by fringed and embroidered Chinese export shawls that achieved worldwide fame when Nicole Kidman wore it to the 1997 Academy Awards ceremony a few weeks later.

Dior's Pin-Ups

Presented at the Musée Guimet (Paris's museum
of Asian art) in the year that saw Hong Kong being
handed over to China, John Galliano's first ready-to-
wear collection for Dior 'lightly plays on the paradox
between history and modernity, yesterday and today,
East and West,' the house declared.

'That collection was inspired by Chinese pin-ups,
Shanghai calendar girls of the 1930s. I'd discovered
these wonderful advertisements for cigarettes, toilet
water [perfume], and other beauty products featuring
beautiful women in tightly fitting *qipaos*. They were
so inspiring,' Galliano told Andrew Bolton. 'The
qipao is already a very sensual garment, but I wanted
to heighten its sensuality further by cutting it on
the bias, which exaggerates the contours of a woman's
body. It produced this natural drape at the knees,
which I amplified in some of the *qipaos*. The fabrics
I used were extremely beautiful: brocades, light silks
with lace inserts, and heavier silks traditionally used
for men's ties and cravats.'

The Eastern inspiration was mixed with the aesthetic
of Hollywood pin-ups: 'the hyper-femininity of the
Jayne Mansfields, the Kim Novaks ... and France's
own famous Brigitte Bardot', who took an exotic
look, with models sporting lacquered red nails and
Diana Vreeland-style rouged cheeks.

Revisiting Christian Dior's 'famous draped bow
[see, for example, p. 78], which now accompanies
very short and saucy little dresses with balloon
skirts' (such as 'Diorzhou', the Ming-blue bustier
dress opposite), and incorporating mandarin collars,
obi-style bows and belts as well as slit tunics and
kimono cuts, the collection launched 'the L-line –
an innovative and skilful cut that makes skirts and
sheath dresses drape asymmetrically, while keeping
the silhouette fluid,' as the collection notes stated.

Opening with the shapely and ultra-short 'Marilyn'
suit (a powder-pink basket-weave wool 'Bar' jacket
trimmed with fringing and worn with a matching
bias-cut woollen crepe dress with pearled mandarin
collar, shown opposite), the collection was divided
into five parts: 'Dior's little sweetheart pin-ups'
('ingenues, often in pastels, mini-skirts, fur boleros');
'Dior's haughty, smouldering and venomous vamp
pin-ups' ('regal, aristocratic, with a penchant for
black tuxedos, shades of plum and orchids'); 'Dior's
imperial pin-ups' ('Parisienne, exotic and colourful');
'Dior's bohemian muse pin-ups' (featuring 'Juliet',
a jade-coloured crepe evening dress embroidered with
poppies; right); and, finally, 'Dior's lacquered pin-ups'
('voluptuous, passionate: a red kabuki star busting
out of her seams').

Mata Hari in Bagatelle

Unveiled on a hot summer's day in the Jardins
de Bagatelle, this romantic collection was inspired
by the figure of Mata Hari. 'Not the spy trapped
by intrigue and lies but the sensual image of the
exotic Indian dancing girl, with all the suppleness
of a panther in her diamond-incrusted bra,' read
the collection notes. 'Mata Hari incarnates just
as much the Edwardian Belle Epoque, with its
taste for arabesques, corsets, laces, embroidered
silks, faded colours and exacerbated femininity
as she does India with its splendour and intriguing
mysteries.'

In keeping with the house's long tradition of
taking inspiration from artists and paintings,
Galliano intermingled the figure of his imagined
Mata Hari with the work of some of the leading
artists of her time, the Belle Epoque, the era that
had so influenced Christian Dior himself.

The collection opened with a section entitled
'The Edwardian Raj Princesses Chez Dior', which
saw 'Neo-Hindou Edwardian taste' reinvent the
emblematic 'Bar' jacket, which was revisited through
the new 'pyramid line' (see p. 273). A dramatic cut
that creates 'an upward movement from behind
up to the neck and is sometimes transformed into
a throwaway collar-cape effect, a stole-cape or even
a big blanket collar, all on the shoulders', this new
line was 'directly inspired by the Ndebele women
who traditionally envelop themselves majestically
in blankets'. The strictly tailored and corseted
silhouettes were accessorized with maharajah-inspired
jewels (created by Goossens) so monumental that
the earrings were in fact attached to hidden metal
Alice bands that supported their weight.

Next came 'Mucha-Inspired Art Nouveau Artists'
Muses', with 'the exotic yet triumphant femininity
of the slinky curves naturally reminding us
of Sarah Bernhardt, the muse of Art Nouveau,
and more particularly of Alphonse Mucha'. The
famous actress lent her name to an evening dress
embellished with jet-embroidered bouquets, a tulle
ruff and peacock feathers designed to evoke the style
of Art Nouveau stained glass (p. 274, bottom left).

'Exotic Queens As Fashion Victims' was next,
featuring 'Reine Ranavalona III de Madagascar'
with its Chantilly-lace shawl (p. 275, top right),
followed by 'Toulouse Lautrec's Little Parisiennes'
(see p. 275, bottom left), 'Lovely Ladies at Evenings
Chez Klimt' (including the flaming 'Theodora'
with its dramatic Montgolfier sleeves, bias-cut satin
skirt and taffeta waist-cincher; right), 'Mata Hari's
Dancers' (featuring invisible tulle body suits
embroidered with Indian jewelry motifs; see p. 272,
right) and, finally, 'Bronze Princesses At The Ball
of the Century' (see opposite, top left).

'In a Boudoir Mood'

John Galliano moved to the Carrousel du Louvre
(the official location of the Paris collections)
to present his second ready-to-wear collection
for the house. Two vast halls were turned into
an extravagant Belle Epoque mansion for the
occasion, 'with back projection of gilded walls
and high windows overlooking manicured parkland,'
as Colin McDowell reported in *The Sunday Times*.
'The boudoir, bathroom, dining hall and billiard
room were all recreated down to the last detail
with antique furniture, including a rococo bed,
hastily removed clothes tossed on chaises longues
and rose petals floating in the bath water.'

Models moved from one 'room' to the next,
staging *tableaux vivants* as they went, encouraged
by the designer to give life to the particular
'character' each had been assigned, in a *mise en
scène* which, according to fashion historian Caroline
Evans, 'recalled the wax tableaux behind glass
of the 1900 Exposition Universelle in Paris [the
first to feature contemporary fashion] with their
simulations of the luxury and extravagance of
haute couture'.

Titled 'In a Boudoir Mood', the collection was
imagined for a woman who 'rediscovers her
naturally light and graceful body in a supple-
looking silhouette and loves living in the softest
lingerie she has decided to show off even for
the day,' read the collection notes, developing
the lingerie theme Galliano had touched on
in his first Dior ready-to-wear collection even
further (see p. 268, top right).

The collection, hailed by *The Times* as the
designer's 'most wearable yet', focused particularly
on evening dresses, many of which revisited the
themes of the designer's previous haute couture
collection (see p. 270), from luxurious Raj-inspired
jewelry to light silk mermaid-line bias-cut dresses
embellished with Art Deco motifs.

'A Poetic Tribute to the Marchesa Casati'

John Galliano invited his audience to Paris's Opéra Garnier for a lavish spectacle inspired by the highly eccentric muse, heiress and arts patron Marchesa Luisa Casati, 'a great Italian lady from the beginning of this century, whose extraordinary personality ... made her famous throughout Europe,' explained the collection notes. Known for her flaming red hair, smoky eye makeup and snow-white skin, she 'transformed her life into an oriental tale, living in a Venetian palace surrounded by monkeys, exotic birds, greyhounds and a snake she wore as a necklace'.

Painted by artists such as Giovanni Boldini, Kees van Dongen and Augustus John, the Marchesa, who declared she wanted 'to be a living work of art', also captivated poet Gabriele D'Annunzio, who nicknamed her 'Coré' (after the maiden who was abducted by the god of hell, Hades, to become his wife and queen of the underworld), and counted artist and Ballets Russes costume designer Léon Bakst among her friends.

Accompanied by a cascade of rose petals on the grand marble staircase where it appeared, the first ensemble – baptized 'Maria Luisa (dite Coré)' – was 'a black crinoline dress so vast that fashion editors ducked as it moved past', to quote *The Times* (see p. 285, top right).

Six different 'acts' followed. Act I was titled 'A pastoral, Sèvres-porcelain-style story', inspired by the small Trianon-influenced palace where the Marchesa used to live, and revisiting 'the 18th-century neo-Versailles taste for ... exquisite little painted white porcelain shepherdesses' in a series of white and pastel day ensembles accessorized with porcelain medallions.

Act II, 'English story in a country garden', saw an abundance of roses and foliage adorn ensembles with names such as 'Sissinghurst' and 'Garsington'. Act III, 'Story of a voyage in first class', presented perfectly cut travel suits and travel dresses teamed with huge creamy veiled boater hats, followed by a succession of gold lamé tango dresses with striking folds and gathers in Act IV ('Lascivious story to a tango tune'), and richly embroidered Poiret-inspired 'pyramid-line Ballets-Russes kimonos' with high funnel collars in Act V ('Story of an Orientalist encounter with Bakst').

For the final act ('Story of a fancy-dress ball at the Palazzo dei Leoni'), Galliano recreated the Marchesa Casati's own 'Pulcinella' dress (designed for her by Bakst; see p. 283, bottom), and closed the collection with a grandiose light blue ball dress with hooped crinoline on which tiny pastel-coloured butterfly-shaped confetti were promptly showered for a spectacular finale (see p. 285).

'Sportswear on High Heels'

Revisiting his signature Edwardian silhouette
and high Maasai necklaces, as well as the Poiret-
inspired shapes of 1910s opera coats that he had
reinterpreted in his previous collection for the house
(see p. 280), John Galliano added a new element into
the mix: sportswear.

More precisely, he added the *doudoune*, or quilted
down jacket, around which he built his collection,
reinterpreting the highly practical garment in
luxurious fabrics and acid colours, trimming it
with dramatic fur or fringing. It's 'sportswear on
high heels', the designer declared to describe this
new ready-to-wear collection, which, according
to *The Times*, 'moved out of the boudoir ... and
into the street', even though it retained a healthy
dose of fantasy.

Galliano was inspired by the work of Italian
photographer Tina Modotti, who in 1913 travelled
from her native country to California, where she
became involved in the city's arts scene before
moving to Mexico City in the early 1920s. In Mexico,
Modotti soon joined a community of cultural and
political 'avant-gardists' that included Frida Kahlo
and Diego Rivera, documenting the nascent Mexican
mural movement and capturing local peasants and
workers in her lyrical images.

'That's why we did a touch of Mexico,' said milliner
Stephen Jones, who created a series of wide-brimmed
tin hats with Mexican motifs, while the influence
of Central American folk dress could also be detected
in the brightly coloured patchwork designs that
adorned several jackets.

'A Voyage on the Diorient Express, or the story of the Princess Pocahontas Collection'

Bursting through a curtain of orange paper on a platform at the Gare d'Austerlitz, the 'Diorient Express' steam train and its thirty-three models (plus accompanying American Indian warriors) made a dramatic entrance.

Having previously imagined a meeting between Princess Pocahontas and Wallis Simpson for his John Galliano autumn/winter 1996–1997 collection, this time the designer set out to combine 'a spirit of Renaissance splendour with the lithe grace of American Indians'.

'All aboard for Vanity Fair, the Silk Route, the Three Wise Men's caravan loaded with gold, incense and myrrh, the Embassies of China and Persia, Moorish splendours and the field of the Cloth of Gold, where the Valois, Francis I and the Tudor, Henry VIII, jousted together in lavish rivalry,' proclaimed the collection notes.

'Bon voyage! To Medici Princesses, their heads held high with frilly maiden-white ruffs, en route for the French Court, escorted by their flirtatious pageboys in cape and culottes, their weary confessors and daunting chaperones. Bon voyage! To boot-shod musketeers who in one gallant sweep raise their wide-brimmed feathered hats to startled black-clad missionaries passing by.'

And, of course, 'To the Princess Pocahontas who hides her exotically romantic allure in her private wagon, decorated with intensely coloured and symbolic pattern embroidered doeskin in memory of the hide tunics of her youth, when she ran free as the wind in the forests of Virginia... This is her first trip on the Diorient Express and the first journey of an American Indian to the England of James I.'

Inspired by 16th-century aristocratic dress, Galliano presented the 'doublet-Bar' line for jackets, magnificent Henry VIII coats (including a luxurious white doeskin creation trimmed with an ermine collar and embroidered all over with oak leaf, acorn, strawberry and flower appliqué motifs emblematic of the Elizabethan era; see right and opposite, bottom right), intricate pinking and slashing, voluminous furs (from fox and sable to the large mink collar of the 'Chevalier Vison Futé' ensemble pictured overleaf), and long-sleeved silk evening dresses inspired by portraits of Renaissance princesses (in particular by the works of painter Lucas Cranach the Elder; see p. 293, top left), accessorized with heavy necklaces borrowed from the jewelry of the Miao people of China for a truly global world tour on the Diorient Express.

DIORIENT EXPRESS

Communists & Constructivists

After the Diorient Express, John Galliano took
a trip on the Trans-Siberian Railway (albeit a
scaled-down one, presented in the Christian Dior
headquarters on the avenue Montaigne), drawing
inspiration from the Russian avant-garde as well
as the Chinese Red Army.

'For the first half of the collection,' Galliano told
Andrew Bolton, 'I was looking at Chinese military
uniforms – the colour, the gold accents. The touches
of red, the small red beads and silk armbands, came
from the uniforms of the Red Guards, Mao's young
disciples, [but] the pleats came from Mariano
Fortuny, and they were executed in the lightest
of silks.'

The finale, however, drew on the geometric motifs
of the work of Ukrainian-born artist Sonia Delaunay,
and called to mind both Kazimir Malevich's stark
Suprematist compositions and the aesthetic of
Russian Constructivism – in particular, the striking
1920s clothing designs of Varvara Stepanova and
Alexander Rodchenko.

Surrealist Couture

John Galliano presented a surrealism-influenced
collection in the Dior salons to a strictly limited
audience (with no more than sixty people admitted
at a time, presentations were held throughout
the day to allow guests to 'enjoy the collection
on a more intimate scale').

'The mood is surrealistic, in the way that Dali
and Cocteau understood it – witty and startling
at times but always romantic,' Galliano declared.
'You'll see daywear with gala moments dropped
in. The tailoring mixes male and female sensualities
as well as *trompe l'œil* effects – often in the same
garment. The spirit is eclectic and the mood
monochromatic with a lot of fantasy thrown in.'

'I've been thinking about the photographs of
Angus McBean and Man Ray, whose experiments
with light playing around the body and redefining
its contours are fascinating. I've taken the mood
and interpreted it in the softest fabrics to bring
about the same poetic qualities. The gentle side
to surrealism in the society portraits by Madame
Yevonde also appeals to me. She convinced her
sitters that they were goddesses such as Athena
or Diana the huntress – and, believe it or not,
Madame Yevonde came from Streatham in South
London, just like me.'

In Modigliani's Studio

In keeping with Galliano's strongly art-influenced previous collection for the house (see p. 300), his latest creations were presented in a Dior-grey set filled with empty frames and blank canvases to evoke the atmosphere of an artist's studio.

The artist in question was Amedeo Modigliani, and the collection was inspired both by the rich hues of his paintings and his many portraits of his young mistress, the artist Jeanne Hébuterne (such as the 1918–19 *Jeanne Hébuterne with Yellow Sweater*). Like Modigliani in his time, Galliano also looked to 'subtle African influences embodied by the wooden fertility sculptures from the Dogon tribe of Mali', which he mixed with the symbols of Dior 'to deliver his own very personal vision of sportswear for Dior for the year 2000, where knit plays a major part,' as the collection notes stated.

The 'Bar' suit was reinterpreted in stretchy coloured knit, and Galliano also offered up 'stunning voluptuous sweaters, pull-overs with huge rolled necklines, loose-back closed cable-knit cardigans and sailor-collared coats with heavily textured African patterned motifs, worn over everything from long skirts to evening dresses or worked into mermaid dresses'.

The knitwear was feminized by details such as 'fringes, feathery effects, bobbles of Aran stitches, giant witch-balls, ribbed stitching, mink knitting', and even a glitter knit for evening ensembles, presented alongside day dresses 'with elegantly reversible short or long A-line jackets worn over a long pencil skirt'.

The 'Matrix' Collection

Presented at the Orangerie in the Palace of
Versailles, Galliano's last Dior collection before
the millennium defied expectations: there were
no lavish sets and no luxurious reinterpretations
of Louis XIV dress, but instead a narrow, silvery
catwalk covered with waterbed pillows on which
the first look to emerge was a beret-wearing urban
warrior dressed in black (right; less than a year
after the designer's Red Army-inspired designs,
see p. 296).

'A meteoric wind is blowing through this
New Generation Dior Collection straight out
of the Matrix where the real and the virtual are
perpetually co-existent,' read the collection notes.
Quoted as a 'deep inspiration', the 1999 film was
revisited in a series of monochrome (black, lime
or bright red) ensembles in leather, PVC, rubberized
linen, mohair or mink.

Then a new act started, and the designer sent
down 'the wardrobe of the English aristocrat
who dresses at Savile Row, goes hunting in
Scotland, is keen on sailing, fly fishing, horse
riding, mountain climbing and whose clothes
have been appropriated, pulled apart and
recontextualized, to dress a multi-faceted woman
who delights in Gainsborough's fresh elegance
and the richness of precious Persian miniatures'
(the latter inspiring intricately embroidered
and beaded silk tulle dresses).

Galliano's theme was 'the female warrior, the
huntress, from sinister and shiny *Waterworld*
deviants with black-rimmed eyes ... to Inca
goddesses and African huntresses, via 18th-century
ladies ready to ride to hounds but pausing to be
painted by Reynolds, Raeburn and Gainsborough,'
wrote Colin McDowell in *The Sunday Times*. 'The
mood swung from menacing to pastoral and then
to extraterrestrial, with the last outfit landing
complete with open parachute', proudly held aloft
by an Amazonian Carmen Kass wearing a red
sequined plastic and satin evening dress (see p. 315).

'Contemporary and innovative yet always
infinitely romantic, the Dior woman brilliantly
masters the modernity of third-millennium
elegance,' the house proclaimed.

'Logomania'

'Couture blaxploitation, logos-a-go-go,
leather-clad revolutionaries, whip-toting modern
courtesans – where else but at Dior?' *Vogue* asked.
'John Galliano's romp started with a series of wildly
sexy denim looks reminiscent of a glammed-out
Foxy Brown: knee-high lace-up logo boots, foulard
tops made out of Dior's signature print, frayed
microskirts and supersexy tan leather trousers.'

Inspired in part by the style of Lauryn Hill
(whose latest album, 'The Miseducation of Lauryn
Hill', provided the soundtrack for the first part
of the show), Galliano resurrected the Dior-logo
print from the house's archive and used it to cover
spiral-cut slashed denim mini-dresses and matching
denim boots (later worn by Beyoncé Knowles in
the video for Destiny's Child's 'Jumpin' Jumpin'').

Equestrian motifs ran through the collection,
from the iconic 'Saddle' bag to gold-buckle patterns
printed on chiffon tops and silk scarves, buckled
leather boots, whips, and fantastical starry satin
evening dresses that echoed the bright motifs
of horse-racing jockey shirts.

'Les Clochards'

Described by *Women's Wear Daily* as 'one of the
most controversial fashion shows ever staged',
this haute couture collection was inspired by
Paris's homeless population, the tradition of the
fancy dress 'Rag Balls' (where the aristocracy
and rich bourgeoisie dressed 'up' in the garb
of destitutes and beggars), and Diane Arbus's
Untitled photographs of the mentally ill.

'I wanted to turn couture on its head,' John
Galliano later declared about his collection,
for which the programme notes contained only
the following line, from Oscar Wilde's preface to
his *Picture of Dorian Gray*: 'All art is at once surface
and symbol. Those who go beneath the surface
do so at their peril.'

Silk taffeta was printed with newspaper pages
(Dior headlines from the *International Herald Tribune*
– an echo of the newspaper print first launched
in high fashion in the 1930s by Elsa Schiaparelli,
who had got the idea from observing Danish
fishwives twisting newspaper pages into small
hats), and the designer 'sent out frayed beauties
with Charlie Chaplin eyes and hobo trinkets
dangling from their waists,' as Cathy Horyn
reported for *The New York Times*.

Developing 'the deconstructed theme of his last
shows ... the clothes were twisted back to front
and inside out, so the labels and linings were all
exposed,' Horyn continued. They were followed
by a series of white ensembles tied with strings
and rope to echo straitjackets, and teetering
ballerinas.

For the finale, the designer offered up hand-
painted silk taffeta and silk tulle evening
dresses inspired by the work of Egon Schiele.
'I just loved the idea of this wonderful muse
escaping from the canvas and trying to evoke
that illustrative line, actually using real paints
and emulsion on the toile, then layering it with
tulle to give these very painterly strokes to the
dress,' Galliano explained.

'It was pure performance art: Diane Arbus
photographs brought to life,' wrote Tamsin
Blanchard, while Cathy Horyn concluded: 'What
Mr Galliano is really attempting to do by showing
clothes in such a seemingly deranged manner
is to deconstruct the myth of Dior.'

'Fly Girls'

Building on the themes of his previous ready-to-wear
collection for the house (see p. 316), John Galliano
created a deliberately decadent collection, bringing
back denim (here in tie & dye versions), logomania
and the saddle bag, to mention just a few elements.

Held in the Théâtre National de Chaillot, on a
gold mirrored catwalk, the collection was divided
into three parts. The first 'takes its influence from
American rappers, brassy and fun,' stated the house,
'the second a romantic ballet theme inspired by
the ballerinas of the haute couture collection, and
the third … sexy lingerie dresses in satin and lace,
perfect for the Oscars and Cannes Film Festival'.

Newsprint, featured heavily in the house's previous
collection (see p. 318), was also revisited: the *Christian
Dior Daily*, created for the occasion, with headlines
about Galliano himself, appeared on 'bias-cut
flounced mousseline or silk jersey dresses, lingerie,
tiny chinchilla blousons and micro saddle bags'.

The Dior logo and 'CD' initials were also used
prominently on accessories, from 'CD' bit-buckles
on spike-heeled boots to 'thick identity Dior chain
necklaces, diamond and gilded CD buttons and
"D-I-O-R" rings'.

'Freud or Fetish'

After his previous, highly controversial haute
couture collection for the house (see p. 318),
John Galliano was inspired by Sigmund Freud
and the idea of fetishism, basing this new collection
on an imaginary letter from Freud to Carl Jung
that read: 'Recently I glimpsed an explanation
for the case of fetishism. So far it concerns only
clothes, but it is probably universal.'

'I believe M. Christian Dior was the first true
fetishist designer,' Galliano told *The Telegraph*.
'He had an Oedipus complex, he was in awe of
his mother and his New Look was full of fetish
symbolism. You only have to look at the high
heels, the corsets which emphasised the bust and
waist, the big skirts which emphasised the hips.'
He added to Suzy Menkes, 'I am trying to symbolize
what fetishism evokes in the psychology of clothing.'

Divided into three parts, the collection opened
with scenes of an Edwardian society wedding –
'I was the mother of the bride, but it was a rather
unhappy family, very grand, very aristocratic, very
embittered by life,' explained model Marisa Berenson
(opposite, right) – with unexpected twists: the
'bishop' officiating was dressed in an embroidered
and padded New Look robe (opposite, below left),
while the bridegroom had his hands tied behind
his back by a pearl necklace (right).

Then the 'nightmare' sequence started: 'that feeling
of this young child looking through the keyhole and
seeing what the real world was about, that mummy
was sleeping with the chauffeur and the chauffeur
was having it off with papa, and this, well, this
is one of his nightmares,' Galliano declared. Figures
were 'culled as much from childish nightmares as
from the sexual fantasies of supposedly straight-
laced bourgeois Vienna,' wrote fashion historian
Caroline Evans.

The figures included a bejewelled French maid
wearing a black embroidered dress and lace apron
over a red silk corset (p. 331, top left), a fantastical
'horse-woman' with leather dress, boater, saddle
and tail (p. 331, bottom), and a subtly sinister
Marie-Antoinette-like doll (p. 330, top left, with
a red cross marking her white neck, and an antique
faille dress hand-embroidered with bloody guillotines
and decapitated sheep's heads among the flower
motifs) suddenly come to life.

The final part moved from childhood nightmares
to adult S&M and bondage sexual fantasies: a model
coiffed with a barrister's wig holding a noose around
her neck (p. 332, bottom right), a nun with her hands
tied by rosary beads (p. 332, top), and 'an Edwardian
beauty in a red satin topper led in on a leash by
a black and white Leigh Bowery lookalike [p. 333,
top left],' noted Caroline Evans – a reminder of
Galliano's roots in London clubland.

Ripped & Zipped

A clear break from the romanticism of Galliano's previous designs for the house, this collection embraced punk, pop, Americana, collage and camouflage, while taking his efforts at deconstruction further than before.

'Let's talk about why John Galliano's cold, shallow, lurid, brutal, hysterical show for Dior today was absolutely dead on,' wrote Cathy Horyn in *The New York Times*. 'This collection was the real thing. It had the raw authenticity, the lubricity, of garage couture. When the first models started trampling out ... you could barely take it all in: the fishnets and banana clips, the beaten brown leather of a wrap skirt, the stiletto biker boots, the tops covered with car and motor-oil patches. It had irony ... but also a pop sense of composition, of taking things apart and rearranging them in a new form.' And, indeed, the designer explained that each piece in the collection could be zipped to another, 'so you can create your own look'.

'His strange, mutant clothes – pitting the front of a romantic dress against a denim-clad backside – were scarred with zippers,' wrote Suzy Menkes. 'They circled the body, threatening to open up windows on the naked torso and allowing the skimpy garments to morph into different shapes... The clothes on the runway seemed like sampling in music ... then suddenly came a complete aria of quiet beauty, as in a terry toweling coat splattered with flowers.'

Commercial elements were not forgotten: the names of Dior fragrances were emblazoned across dozens of ensembles, and the designer presented the new Dior 'Cadillac' handbag complete with patent-leather chassis, door-handle clasp and shoulder straps fixed by a mini 'CD'-embossed steering wheel.

Wonder Woman

'"Daughter, rouse yourself! Burst your bonds of mind and body!" read a 1950s Wonder Woman cartoon strip by William Moulton Marston that was tacked onto John Galliano's inspiration board at Dior,' *Vogue* reported. Galliano's re-imagined story of Wonder Woman as a proto-feminist icon was the narrative that structured this collection.

'The show opening is about repressed postwar women,' the designer explained, 'but through the clothes you can see hints of the liberated women they will become.' Straitlaced secretaries strutted down the catwalk in deconstructed and offbeat ensembles, followed by 1950s housewives wearing hand-painted and embroidered silk organza and tulle dresses decorated with naïve domestic motifs, from cups of tea to cleaning products.

Suddenly Wonder Woman appeared, in multiple incarnations, 'chasing away the frustrated moms in their ballooning maternity tulle dresses,' Suzy Menkes reported, embodying 'sexy superheroines [and showing] breathtaking workmanship on the customized denim biker jackets'.

For the final part of the show, Galliano's Wonder Woman retired to her birthplace, the women-only Paradise Island, where she could 'enjoy the sun in ravaged Grecian dresses, ancient bits of fur and dusty Mad Max boots,' *Vogue* concluded.

Technicolour Rave

John Galliano proposed a fluoro-coloured, rave-inspired collection born out of a kaleidoscope of references that included the films *Fight Club* and *Snatch*, gypsies, Irish boxers and 1960s hippies.

'Dior is exploding in a young and colourful blast of optimism, fantasy and fun, dressing you up with happiness,' read the programme notes. 'Here is the youth of the "Rêve parties" in baggy trousers, chiffon dresses and silk tops... And there's a brand new star in the accessories hit parade: the "Boom Box" bag, oversized and cloned from street rappers' giant blasters.'

'Details and accessories are reinvented freely, swiped here and there from rap, Wall Street, the boxing ring or travelling people. Itinerary of a spoiled child, who, from Ireland to the banks of the Danube, appropriates and remixes all the fashions she encounters to reinvent her own elegance.'

'Barbie goes to Tibet'

Building on the fluorescent colours and fighting
spirit of his previous collection for the house
(see p. 342), John Galliano opened this haute
couture collection with a series of ensembles he
called 'Rebel Chic' – 'paramilitary references mixed
with non-specific Eastern exoticism ... rugged with
delicate, Amelia Earhart meets Arabian Nights,
discordant pieces in harmonious layerings,' as
Women's Wear Daily described it. 'I put an emphasis
on separates, treating couture like you would
sportswear,' the designer told *Vogue*.

The second act of the collection evoked the
atmosphere of hippie-chic Goa with brightly
coloured hand-painted pleated silk chiffon dresses
teamed with hand-painted bikinis – 'a little bit
1970s, Zandra Rhodes, those looser shapes, Bill
Gibb, a very kind of London vibe,' Galliano told
Colin McDowell, 'painted by Georges Krivoshey,
and tie-dyed too.'

Inspired by both Tibetan imagery and the aesthetic
of larger-than-life plastic Barbie dolls, the collection's
finale presented a succession of awe-inspiring
patchwork puffa coats, plastic embroidered jackets,
embroidered and re-embroidered denim-and-fur
trousers, and silk kimono shirts.

The bow-like, 'awesome, uncompromising, almost
menacing' shape of the collection's most striking
piece (p. 351, top left) was inspired by the costumes
of Japanese kyōgen theatre, which captured
Galliano's imagination. Gravity-defying, it
nevertheless remained light – 'that's the magic of
Raphael at the haute couture ateliers,' the designer
explained; 'this was then all done layer by layer and
then they were decorated by different embroiderers,
and you could see hair clips and things, and this
lovely – almost like cellophane – packaged-doll
vibe which I thought was really charming.'

'Street Chic'

Continuing to infuse his collections for the house
with a spirit of deconstruction and streetwear,
John Galliano christened this new ready-to-wear
collection 'Street Chic'.

While the collection opened with a series of
romantic bias-cut satin and silk ensembles 'on
a string of models with the powdered and rouged
faces of ill-fated French nobles,' as *Vogue* described
it, they were swiftly followed by 'a pack of tough
LA gangbangers in bandanas and baggy gangsta
trousers' sporting Galliano's new sheer 'tattoo-print'
T-shirts.

Next came a stop in the Middle East with turbans
and diaphanous sarouel trousers, and 'East-meets-
Wild-West numbers with cowgirls in feathered
Stetsons who nonetheless displayed an affinity
for Arabian exotica,' *Women's Wear Daily* reported.

The 'Montaigne' (for Dior's headquarters on the
avenue Montaigne) emblazoned Stetsons played
with the codes of Americana, as did a white Elvis
trouser suit splendidly embroidered with the words
'Memphis or Bust' (see p. 355, right) and 'Christian
Club', before the collection made a final stop south
of the US border with Mexican serape-print bathing
suits and a new 'Havana' print used on everything
from hooded georgette tops to lacquered trousers.

From Russia to Mongolia

After taking inspiration from Tibet for his
previous haute couture collection (see p. 346),
John Galliano transported his audience to Russia
and to Mongolia for this spectacular show.

'It was the result of a magical trip around Russia –
we spent ten days doing research,' the designer
told Andrew Bolton. 'We were backpacking.
We wanted to experience the real Russia... We
went to theatres, ballet schools, and ethnological
museums... The Mongolian costumes [in museum
archives] were extraordinary, heavily layered and
embroidered. Some were made up of seven layers.
They inspired several of the pieces in the
collection.'

Accompanied on the catwalk by Japanese
drummers from the Za Ondekoza troupe,
circus ribbon twirlers in feathered tutus and
even contortionists, the models sported richly
embroidered patchwork denim jackets and silk
coats, multicoloured silk faille dresses and, for
the finale, floor-length embroidered silk taffeta
evening gowns – 'a festival of sensory overload
and wonder,' *Women's Wear Daily* reported.

A Trip to Peru

After Goa and Tibet (see p. 346), Mexico and Cuba
(see p. 352), and Russia and Mongolia (see p. 356),
John Galliano took Dior on a trip to South America,
offering up monumental rainbow Mohawks attached
to Peruvian knitted hats, patchwork skirts, sheepskin
jackets, brightly coloured pom-pom knits and
moccasin boots.

'The clothes were sexily recut from a haul of Indian,
South American, Mongolian and Tibetan materials,'
Vogue's Sarah Mower reported, and teamed, naturally,
with 'the constantly updated Dior Saddle bags'.

'His shows are like elaborate postcards,' Lisa
Armstrong wrote for *The Times*, but 'as well
as trawling continents, Galliano crossed several
decades, including the 1940s, 1950s and 1970s …
[creating] some of the most beautiful clothes shown
on the catwalk anywhere in the past three weeks.'

'New Glamour'

Entitled 'New Glamour', this haute couture collection
took inspiration from the golden days of Hollywood
in the 1940s and the idea of Kate Moss being, as
John Galliano declared, 'today's equivalent of the
great Hollywood glamour icons'. A research trip
took the designer and his collaborators 'through
Los Angeles and Mexico ... [where] they ransacked
movie studio archives for the costumes of Theda Bara
and Marlene Dietrich,' *Vogue* explained. Galliano's
right-hand man, Steven Robinson, told *Women's Wear
Daily*, 'With every outfit, we asked ourselves, "How
would Kate wear it?"'

Galliano presented 'striking mixes of the raw and
the beautiful, the huge and the minuscule, with
a new construction technique based on lathering
hems with feathers and foam as a backing so clothes
are as light as air,' the house stated – perfect for
flying right up over a Marilyn Monroe-esque 'subway
grate' installed on the catwalk in echo to the iconic
Seven Year Itch scene.

The collection made use of a 'colourful and unusual
blend of materials, from unassuming fabrics such
as cotton and denim, to luxurious silk chiffon and
jersey, tulle, taffetas, satin and lace, but also ostrich
feathers, raffia, suede and crocodile leather,' the house
stated, teamed with monumental, showgirl-worthy
feathered headdresses and ultra-high platform shoes.

Showgirls

A ready-to-wear distillation of John Galliano's
Hollywood-inspired haute couture extravaganza
(see p. 366), this collection featured heavy showgirl
makeup, high studded platform shoes, khaki colours
(used here in a series of silk jersey dresses) and an
abundance of ostrich feathers, as well as ultra-short
chiffon parachute dresses, metallic bikinis and new,
fluorescent, collaged Dior prints.

The designer 'displayed accessible versions of the
gargantuan leather jackets, strap-bound leather tubes
and plunging goddess dresses that appeared in his
July couture show,' Sarah Mower wrote for *Vogue*,
adding that 'the method to John Galliano's Dior
madness is no longer in debate'.

China Meets Japan

'It was Asia, but not as we know it,' *Vogue*
reported. For this haute couture collection,
John Galliano was inspired by a recent three-week
trip to China and Japan, where he met the Shaolin
monks and Chinese acrobats he persuaded to come
to Paris to perform on the catwalk alongside his
extraordinary, towering creations.

'My trip to China extended to Japan, so it's a
conflation of both cultures. But, ultimately, it's
just a fantasy. I never set out to re-create anything
literally or religiously. Actually, visiting both
countries in one trip was liberating. I think you
can see this freedom in the collection – in the
textures and in the shapes or volumes of the pieces,'
the designer told Andrew Bolton. 'The shapes were
inspired by Chinese opera costumes, as were the
colours', while the fabrics themselves were more
evocative of Japan.

Galliano played with contrasts, teaming
a gleaming black silk evening dress with a
high-volume, delicately embroidered, pale
pink coat (right), and mixed East and West with
a few silhouettes echoing 19th-century hoops
and crinolines. 'Models, almost completely
submerged in cocooning swaths of brocade, taffeta
and exploding chiffon flounces, teetered along
on vertiginous platforms,' *Vogue* added, in a show
that 'smashed cultural boundaries in a spectacle
of gargantuan theatricality'.

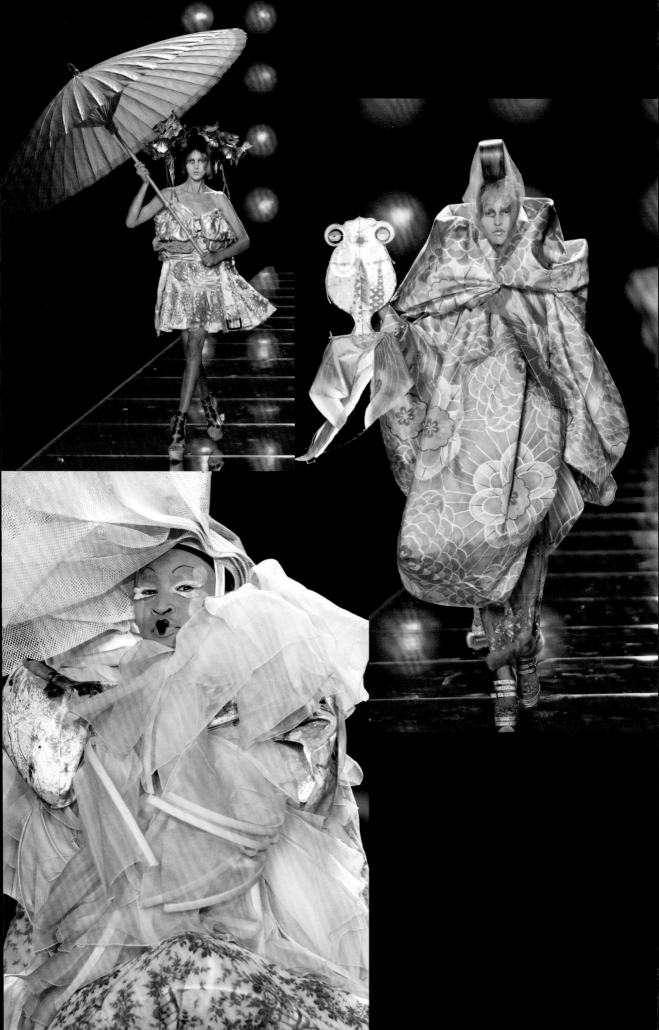

'Hardcore Romance'

Taking inspiration from his previous spectacular haute couture collection (see p. 374), which was 'all about volumes, extreme proportions and dazzling colours,' read the collection notes, 'John Galliano delivers a scaled-down ready-to-wear collection by translating his ideas into wearable clothes and fun accessories: a unique display mixing opposite influences, what he calls "hardcore romance", for sexy, frilly, joyous and colourful clothes.'

Introducing ultra-high platform shoes 'inspired by antique China', as well as the new, crescent-shaped 'The Latest Blonde' bag, the collection mixed rubber, leather, suede, python, knits, silk, organza and chiffon.

Prints – from floral patterns to Japanese and Chinese motifs – were prevalent, as were dramatic ruffles and bunches, box-shape and cube-cut coats and jackets, and even rubber trousers with corset-style lacing: 'a romantic stance playing with the idea of fetishism,' the house declared (a few years after Galliano's fetishism-inspired collection for Dior, see p. 328).

'Creating a New Dance'

Loosely divided into six 'moments' – flamenco,
latino, tango, ballroom, ballet and can-can – this
haute couture collection was entitled 'Creating
a New Dance'. 'A trip through India where
traditional dancers reflect movements found across
the continents in many forms of dance led to the
questioning: why and how did dance evolve? What
makes it so moving, and how does it influence us?'
asked the collection notes.

Incorporating ceremonial African dance, the
dance halls of Jamaica and the technique of Martha
Graham, John Galliano explored the multiple facets
of dance, focusing not only on final performances
but also on 'the feeling captured in the moments
of rehearsal, with its raw energy', quoting the 1969
Sydney Pollack film *They Shoot Horses, Don't They?*
(which depicts a marathon dance competition)
as a key reference.

'It's the denial, passion, discipline and tension that
are so moving,' the designer explained. 'Costumes
suddenly go out the window, it's the reality of the
emotion that is felt.' This became the aim of the
collection: using couture to create 'an abstract,
conceptual interpretation of dance, creating clothes
that themselves take life and dance around the body'.

'The first toiles were separated into literal themes
such as Tango, Flamenco, Ballet, etc. These were
then cut into, to weave the magic into them and
achieve an expression from the materials, feeling
of movement and of immediacy, clothing that clings
and moves with the body. Clothing that looks like
she has been dancing to the point of sheer fatigue
and exhaustion. Some toiles were modified up to
sixteen times to achieve the final results,' the
house stated.

'This collection is a waltz through haute couture
techniques, such as the Cube cut, first used in
the January haute couture collection [see p. 374]
to create three-dimensional flowers that blossom
out of the clothes, and pleating that is held together
with stop cords normally associated with sportswear',
while undergarments 'evoke the rehearsal studio,
where linings coming out, sleeves roughly rolled up,
a T-shirt ripped and knotted expresses the sense
of urgency and spontaneity'.

A Tribute to Marlene

John Galliano chose none other than Hollywood icon Marlene Dietrich as his muse for this collection, albeit with a contemporary twist. 'I tried to imagine if Marlene Dietrich was here today,' Galliano explained. 'She'd be Janis Joplin, she'd be Marianne Faithfull. She'd be Courtney Love. They were the initial inspiration.'

A loyal Dior customer who insisted on Dior costumes for her films ('no Dior, no Dietrich,' she reputedly told even the great Alfred Hitchcock), Dietrich was also the subject of an exhibition at Paris's Palais Galliera fashion museum a few months before the collection.

While her influence was visible in the 1940s-style satin skirt suits and fur stoles that opened the collection, they were contrasted with elements borrowed from lingerie as well as sportswear, and teamed with gypsy tattoo-print tops and stockings that read 'Dior Gitane', 'Hardcore Dior', 'Adiorable' and 'Carmen *hearts* Chris'.

H-Line Pharaohs

John Galliano, freshly returned from a tour
of Egypt that included the Valley of the Kings,
Cairo, Aswan and Luxor, created an haute couture
collection that mixed Ancient Egyptian references
with reminiscences of Christian Dior's own 1950s
'H Line' (see p. 74) and the photographs of Richard
Avedon and Irving Penn to celebrate, as the house
stated, 'the cult of a goddess-like woman and the
supremacy of Elegance'.

Many years after his 'Suzy Sphinx' collection for
his eponymous label (autumn/winter 1997), the
designer worked what he called 'the sphinx line:
elongated, tight, attenuated, but crossed with the
elegance of Avedon and Penn', producing 'a gilded
fantasia that used every treasure available to the
couture ateliers – gold leaf, lapis lazuli-hued snake,
silver lamé, coral beading – to reference everything
from Nefertiti and King Tut to hieroglyphs and
tomb paintings,' *Vogue* reported.

Like the original H line, the silhouette was
'controlled, elongated, with a flat bust and slim,
corseted hips' and expressed through column-sheath
dresses, 'mummy' ribboned dresses, pyramid-shaped
collars, and billowing dresses with hems folded into
lotus-flower shapes.

Flamboyant accessories – from scarab-beetled
earrings and brooches to winged-eagle breast-plates
and turquoise necklaces, pyramid-shaped platform
sandals and shoes festooned with coral and turquoise
ropes of pearls – added the finishing touch.

Art Deco Teddy Boys

In echo to Galliano's Egyptian collection for Dior
a few months earlier (see p. 392), this ready-to-wear
presentation offered up dramatic makeup,
monumental jewelry (including gleaming 'wing'
earrings), pyramid-shaped shawl collars, leopard
prints, and bright yellows, pinks and purples.

Evoking what *Women's Wear Daily* described as
'a post-modern Art Deco feel', the collection was
inspired by Teddy Boy style (the 1950s British
subculture that was partly inspired by the fashions
worn by dandies in the Edwardian period and
closely associated with early rock and roll), given
here a 1910s and 1920s edge.

Referencing the work of fashion illustrator Eduardo
Garcia Benito (who drew covers for *Vogue* and
illustrated luxury publications such as *La Dernière
Lettre Persane* at the beginning of the 20th century),
Galliano mixed signature Teddy Boy platform
creepers and quiffs with exaggerated single-buttoned
cocoon or kimono coats reminiscent of Paul Poiret's
designs (and captured in several of Benito's
illustrations), teamed with a plethora of 'Dior'-
emblazoned accessories.

Empress Sisi

'Vienna, Istanbul – back from a trip in central
Europe, John Galliano proposes his very free vision
for a collection that mixes romantic 19th-century
references, resuscitating Empress Elisabeth ('Sisi')
of Austria, the glamour of 1950s pin-ups and
Zsa Zsa Gabor,' stated the collection notes.

For his most stately haute couture collection yet,
the designer 'put on a regal display of mermaid-
silhouetted robes accessorised with crowns, orbs,
diamonds and long white gloves that made humble
subjects of his A-list audience,' *Vogue* reported.

The most luxurious materials were used: silks,
brocades, moirés, taffeta and velvets, trimmed with
sable, ermine and fox, adorned with peacock feathers
and delicately embroidered or hand-painted with
designs reminiscent of 18th-century motifs inspired
by Sèvres porcelain and Fabergé eggs.

Trompe-l'œil effects such as flesh-coloured bustiers
also peppered the collection, while gravity-defying
pleats and gathers on dramatic evening gowns
showcased the skills of Dior's haute couture ateliers.

Riley, Kirsten, Kate & Gisele

Featuring the new face of Dior, Riley Keough, who
had just been shot by photographer Nick Knight
for the house's latest campaign and walked in the
show, this collection was presented in four sections
'inspired variously by Keough, Kirsten Dunst, Kate
Moss and Gisele Bundchen,' *Women's Wear Daily*
revealed.

Fashion critics hailed the wearability of the
outfits presented, from ecru bouclé and denim suits
evoking the curvy shape of the iconic 'Bar' suit, and
embroidered denim jackets featuring Dior's archive
logo print (first reintroduced by Galliano five years
earlier; see p. 316), to flowing crepe georgette dresses
and printed silk jackets.

Motifs from Galliano's previous collections were
reinterpreted – 'kooky chicks wore multicoloured
jersey tops over transparent tiered chiffon skirts
and striped stockings that disappeared into
Nepalese boots that were a mass of fur pompoms
and ribbons,' *Vogue* wrote, while 'models with wildly
frizzed hair, contained in part by crocheted beanies,
were a glorious homage to the Biba years'. 'These are
real times chez Dior,' *Women's Wear Daily* concluded.

'Andy Warhol is Napoleon in Rags'

'Bob Dylan once said "Andy Warhol is Napoleon in rags" and with that quote the journey began,' John Galliano declared (alluding to the line in Dylan's 'Like a Rolling Stone', the song rumoured to have been inspired by ex-debutante and Factory stalwart Edie Sedgwick), transforming the stage to echo Warhol's Factory with foiled walls and TV sets playing video footage of the fittings.

'After reading Dylan's quote I became fascinated by Edie Sedgwick, Warhol's one-time muse,' Galliano explained. 'The style of this gangly well-bred girl, who lived her fifteen minutes of fame in the fast lane, and in front of Andy's lens, was mesmerising and tragic all at once. Yet, as we delved further into Edie and Warhol's days an unexpected parallel emerged, from another very different era: that of Napoleon's wife, Empress Josephine, and the two eras collided. We have fused together a 1960s adolescent line with the Directoire empire line.'

Exploring the 'reigns' of Josephine and Edie, the story was divided into three acts. First came 'Black', opening with a simple black wool body (right) 'designed to highlight detail, luxury, the Racine jersey, the crocodile accessories,' the designer explained.

The second section was dedicated to red – 'the most flattering colour to wear by candlelight,' according to Christian Dior. 'This section is raw and romantic, inspired by Rembrandt and Cranach,' Galliano continued. 'We've been irreverent with the fabrics, and this is what makes it contemporary. We washed them, scratched them, boiled them, and put these plush grandiose fabrics through torture until only a cobweb, or a frayed wisp of brocade remains, so the gossamers, tulles and chiffons can claw against the cloud-like velvets.'

The final act, 'White', was 'soft and fragile, a delicate silhouette of organza and tulles – embroidery and crystals cascade down dresses like snowflakes. The chandeliers of the emperor's palace inspired the crystals sprinkled through the girls' hair, replacing the caps and berets of earlier. Empire bust lines and Zurburan bows ... embellish dresses worn with coats with Napoleonic collars and the blue-and-white of Delft pottery for touches of colour.' For the finale, as creations became ever more voluminous, so did the size and complexity of the headpieces, with crystal creations based on Chinese embroidery.

'Off-Duty Icons'

Adapting the key references of his previous haute
couture collection (see p. 410) to ready-to-wear
(from Edie Sedgwick-inspired stripes, presented
here in a series of mohair cardigans and jumpers
which opened the show, to empire-line velvet
dresses, berets and crocodile accessories), John
Galliano entitled this collection 'Off-Duty Icons'.
'The silver screen goes "street" as functional
fastenings mix with more poetic influences of
urban glamour,' stated the collection notes.

Aviation was an added influence, with flying
jackets, leather coats and the introduction of the
Dior flight bag (from which swung bright orange
'remove before flight' tags) – 'a mix of sheepskin
and lamé says it all,' Galliano declared.

'I looked at women from other eras and and
imagined how they would dress today,' the
designer said. 'Think of Amelia Earhart in her
flying gear, Garbo, Edith Piaf and other soft-focus
females. Remember Hepburn, Gardner and Harlow
and imagine them followed by the paparazzi.
I wanted modern icons that would make these
looks their own.'

Return to Granville

'This season I was inspired by the representation of Mr Dior's work, in particular the fashion illustrations of René Gruau, Christian Bérard, Cecil Beaton, and the photographs of Lillian Bassman,' John Galliano declared. 'I was also struck, during recent travels in Peru, by surprising similarities in the famous silhouette of Dior's New Look and traditional Peruvian dress.'

The designer sought to reveal all the layers in the construction of haute couture garments, starting with the creation of 'a trompe l'œil nude corset: remoulding the bust and hips into the exaggerated silhouette of a René Gruau illustration. Covering these corsets with a layer of flesh-coloured fabric created a perfect base on which to "illustrate"', the designer explained. 'Now the work of the ateliers could be revealed through the use of transparent tulle, and the techniques of *les petites mains*, which are usually hidden, are exposed in their splendour!'

Celebrating the 100th anniversary of Christian Dior's birth, the collection took its audience on an oneiric journey back to Granville, Dior's childhood home in Normandy. Re-creating the Belle Epoque villa's famous gardens – albeit in a ruined, mysterious and misty version reminiscent of classic RKO horror films – the designer presented a collection divided into ten different acts, each evolving to its own distinct soundtrack.

First came 'Dior's mother: The young Christian Dior observes the strict formality of Edwardian dress'. The opening ensemble, an embroidered tulle dress worn by Erin O'Connor (right) was baptized 'Madeleine' after the couturier's mother, and was followed by 'Jacqueline' (p. 418, top left) and 'Ginette', named for Dior's sisters.

The following section, 'Creation: The Making of a Dress', was described as 'draping, cutting and pinning: M. Dior constructs four dresses on his favourite models' and included deconstructed creations named after Dior's favourite models such as 'Victoire' (p. 418, bottom left).

'Les Directrices', 'Corolle: The New Look' (with 'Carmen', shown opposite, and a succession of Peruvian-inspired corolla-dresses embroidered with multicoloured raffia) and 'Hollywood: The sirens of the silver screen were the super-models of their days' (including 'Vivien' modelled by Eva Herzigova, shown overleaf right) came next, followed by an homage to 'Clients' and 'Debutantes'.

The finale embraced whimsy, with moments titled 'Degas: Margot Fonteyn entertains Christian Dior, Jean Cocteau and Christian Bérard with a Peruvian ballet' (a series of straw-embroidered tulle dresses worn with ballet shoes), 'Catherinettes' (a nod to the tradition, long established in the world of haute couture, for unmarried seamstresses to dress up and wear fantastic hats in yellow and green on Saint Catherine's Day) and, finally, 'Masked Ball', inspired by Peruvian religious colonial paintings from the Cuzco school.

'Dior Nude'

Playing on the nude corsets and construction/
deconstruction effects that characterized his previous
haute couture collection (see p. 416), John Galliano
presented a highly focused ready-to-wear collection
at the newly renovated Grand Palais in Paris. It was
all about 'nude' – 'Dior Nude Black, Dior Nude Lace,
Dior Nude Print, Dior Nude Layering, Dior Nude
Dégradé,' read the collection notes.

According to *Vogue*'s Sarah Mower, the designer
proposed 'a business-like program for maximizing
the potential of a single idea in his last couture
collection: the black-lace-over-nude dress that
Kate Moss wore this summer to the CFDA Awards'.

Opening with printed or jet-embroidered nude
dresses, the collection moved on to offer up
'nude' jackets and trenchcoats with gleaming
white leather 'inside-out' visible seams, followed
by a series of transparent 'nude' dresses decorated
with leather bands that evoked the shape of corsets
and undergarments, and a finale of flowy dégradé
organza and chiffon dresses in shades of 'nude/
green' or 'nude/purple'.

French Revolutions

'Red is the new libertine. Platinum is the new
Marie-Antoinette. Leather is the new luxury.
Veiling is the new seduction. Dior is the new
erotica,' announced the show notes, adding that
John Galliano had found inspiration for this haute
couture collection in a trip around France.

'Corsetry inspiration' first, in the city of Lyon,
where the designer stopped to visit Scandale,
the corsetry manufacturer who had worked with
Christian Dior in the 1950s. Further south, Galliano
explored Arles and met with photographer (and
friend to Picasso) Lucien Clergue, picking up on
'the passion of bullfighting as a key theme'.

Visiting the country home of Marie-Laure de Noailles,
Galliano learned that her mother was a direct
descendant of the Marquis de Sade, which provided
further references for the collection: 'erotica and
libertines', to which the designer added red ('the
colour of passion and Mr Dior's favourite colour').

Presented a few months before the release of Sofia
Coppola's *Marie Antoinette* film, the collection also
echoed the bloody events of the French Revolution:
'clad in huge red capes, cinched-in rough leather
jackets, vast looped-up pannier skirts, laced biker
pants, and shroud-like bindings, his models came
out with their crucifix-festooned necks stencilled
with the date of the revolution: 1789,' Sarah Mower
reported for *Vogue*.

The words 'liberté', 'égalité' and 'fraternité' were
also embroidered on voluminous red linen coats and
jackets, hand-painted on taffeta jackets and leather
trousers, and decorated the white tulle, chiffon and
taffeta finale dress (see p. 427, top right).

'There was a lot of political unrest happening
[this past summer],' the designer told *Vogue*.
'I wanted something bolder and toughened up.
The beat of what's going on.'

'Gothic Chic'

Entitled 'Gothic Chic', this collection (presented
at the Grand Palais) was accompanied by show notes
that read simply 'Bouclé to chiffon. Leather to crin.
Wool to organza. Lurex to taffeta. Lamé to silk.'

John Galliano gave a rock-chick edge to his
revolutionaries of the previous season (see p. 424),
keeping to a similar palette of reds and blacks
with sweeping coats and dresses, but adding
in a multitude of high-impact leather accessories,
from padlocked handbags to statement belts and
thigh-high boots.

'The designer rooted his looks in a core of versatile
pieces – jackets, skirts and coats – that could
swing from lady to vamp,' judged *Women's Wear Daily*,
adding that Galliano 'went mad for skins, working
them in seemingly incongruous combinations: jackets
in leather worked with mink, or at the other end
of the spectrum, tulle, and a high-drama black
bouclé coat encircled with spirals of goat hair
and Mongolian lamb'.

'Planet Botticelli'

'The recent late-night viewing of *Les Visiteurs du Soir* ['The Devil's Envoys'], the classic French film by Marcel Carné set in the 15th century about the arrival of two mysterious minstrels sent by the Devil to bring despair to man, evoked many emotions,' stated the collection notes. 'The beauty of the French actress Arletty in 1940s interpretations of medieval clothes, contrasted with the sinister and alien setting of the castle and gardens in which the plot unfolds, inspired me to look at the work of Renaissance artists such as Botticelli, Leonardo Da Vinci and Jan Van Eyck in a new light – the light of Tuscany in the 15th and 16th centuries,' John Galliano explained.

'Seen through the eyes of someone from a different culture, a different time – almost a different world – the landscapes and people of the High Renaissance seem curiously otherworldly,' he continued. 'The mixed emotions aroused by the film brought to mind the surrealism of Salvador Dali [famous for his use of the lobster motif – a return to surrealism after Galliano's spring/summer 1999 collection for the house; see p. 300], the religious fervour of Joan of Arc, the anarchic energy of punk rock and the iconic glamour of the golden age of Hollywood, experienced by a stranger in a strange land ... the dream of Dior Haute Couture on Planet Botticelli.'

'Back to Basics'

To the sound of Christina Aguilera's 'Back to
Basics', John Galliano presented a very pure and
soft collection in Dior's essential grey tones, marched
down the catwalk by an army of short-haired Joan
of Arc incarnations, echoing the designer's medieval-
inspired collection for the house a few months earlier
(see p. 430).

'We were still taking inspiration from the haute
couture collection,' Galliano explained, 'but
working it in a much more abstracted manner –
really breaking it down, controlling it, no emotion.
For me it was a very exciting way. I'm a very
emotional, Latin person, so it was new territory
for me; I loved it.'

'His spring message was concise: a smart, discreet
suit for day, a beautifully draped dress for night,'
wrote *Women's Wear Daily*. 'Despite their aura of
reserve courtesy of subtle, neutral-toned fabrics,
the suits bore considerable interest: an arm slit on
one, a bold rounded shoulder on another and often,
a measure of tone-on-tone embroidery defining the
jacket' – with slashes and armour details translated
from the haute couture collection – accessorized
with small chain-handled handbags.

Madame Butterfly

Marking John Galliano's ten-year anniversary
at the house, the haute couture collection was
inspired by *Madame Butterfly*, Giacomo Puccini's
famous opera, which tells the story of the young
geisha girl Ciocio-san ('ciocio' is the Japanese
word for 'butterfly') and her ill-fated affair with
the American lieutenant Pinkerton, who abandons
her shortly after their wedding.

Presented on a striking set by Michael Howells
complete with monumental Dior-grey chairs
(making the models look doll-size), oversized cherry
blossoms and revolving mirrors, the collection
echoed the famous story through clothes.

After 'East-meets-West' New Look-inspired suits
such as the intricately pleated embroidered pink
silk gazar suit baptized 'Konnichi-Kate' (right) that
opened the collection, Galliano told the tale 'of the
girl in the fields, the raw simple life – [with] natural
fabrics, linens and straws,' Camilla Morton explained
for *Vogue* UK, with sumptuous embroidered dresses
and coats, hand-painted dégradé silk pieces, and
a delicate hand-painted and embroidered linen
coat decorated with a motif derived from Hokusai's
Great Wave (overleaf).

Next came a new act inspired by geishas, with
ensembles 'named after the notorious women
from Gilbert and Sullivan's *Mikado*,' Camilla Morton
pointed out, such as the embroidered white silk
jacket 'Ko-Ko-San' (p. 441, bottom), followed
by the bright orange and turquoise silk gazar
'Satsuma-San' evening dress (p. 441, top right),
before the focus turned to Madame Butterfly's
samurai father with dark and angular crocodile
creations.

'Kimonos, obis, and geisha makeup were Diorified,
transformed into delicate translations of New Look
peplum suits and full-skirted dance dresses,' Sarah
Mower reported. 'Each look sprouted yet more
miraculous planes of origami folding, their stiff
geometries creating necklines like flowers or hovering
birds' – none more impressive than the white silk
dress that closed the show (p. 443), worn by Shalom
Harlow, ten years after she walked in Galliano's
debut show for Dior (see p. 262, top right).

'It doesn't feel like 10 years – but everything I have
done was in it – including Mr Dior,' Galliano told
Suzy Menkes, who hailed the collection as 'his most
beautiful yet for Dior'.

Furs & Pleats

Set against Michael Howells's monumental
white staircase (designed to evoke that of
Christian Dior's childhood home at Granville),
the collection managed to translate the intricate
Japanese-inspired references and techniques
of Galliano's previous haute couture show
(see p. 438) for ready-to-wear, from origami
folding and gravity-defying pleats to elegant
draping, tiered skirts, striking headpieces and
bright colours.

The designer threw a new element into the mix:
fur, for a very 1940s, Joan Crawford look. It was
'virtually a camp-fabulous Hollywood spectacular,'
wrote *Vogue*'s Sarah Mower, 'like a pumped-up 2007
remake of *The Women* (directed by George Cukor
in 1939; ever a fashion favorite), but this time played
out in full glorious purple, pistachio, electric blue,
and fuchsia, rather than black and white'.

Accessories took pride of place, with woven
leather bags and delicately laced platform shoes,
and Galliano chose 'the most exquisite of materials
– silks, suede, leather, python, croc and fur, fur
and more fur,' *Women's Wear Daily* reported, hailing
the collection as 'a brilliant blockbuster, a glorious
celebration of the grand and glamorous'.

'Le Bal des Artistes'
(The Artists' Ball)

John Galliano looked back to the young
Christian Dior's days as an enthusiastic art gallery
owner (before he started working in fashion) for
this anniversary collection presented at the Orangerie
in Versailles (years after Galliano's landmark 'Matrix'
collection; see p. 310) on a monumental, 130-metre-
long catwalk punctuated with 'tableaux' sets created
by Michael Howells.

'To celebrate the sixtieth anniversary of the house
of Christian Dior,' Galliano declared, 'we explored
Mr Dior's first collection, not of fashion, but of
his favourite artists. Using the spirit of the Neo-
Romantic artists his gallery represented, we have
created the ultimate Bal des Artistes as a tribute
to the memory of Steven Robinson. This season
each look evokes the essence of a great master in
art history. The cut, silhouette and embellishment
of each outfit is led by the spirit of each artist's
style, referencing their inspirations and techniques.'

Detecting an elegiac tone in the collection, *Vogue*'s
Sarah Mower noted that 'the underlying mood was
of respectful homage to two men who devoted their
lives to fashion and died too young: Christian Dior
himself and Galliano's chief designer, Steven
Robinson, who tragically passed away in April
while working toward this collection'.

Opening, fittingly, with a reinterpretation 'inspired
by Irving Penn' of the famous 1947 'Bar' suit, worn
by Gisele Bündchen (right), the collection paid
homage to the work of fashion's most famous
illustrators, from Eric (opposite, top left) to René
Gruau (p. 450, left), Christian Bérard (p. 450, right)
and Jean Cocteau (opposite, right), as well as Picasso
(opposite, bottom left) and great painters from across
Europe: the Impressionists, Sargent, Fragonard,
Watteau, Spanish and Dutch masters, the Pre-
Raphaelites and many more. The finale was dedicated
to the artists of the Renaissance, including Botticelli
(p. 452, bottom left), Caravaggio (channelled by Linda
Evangelista on p. 452, top right) and Titian (p. 453).

After the first act of the collection unfolded,
accompanied by live singing from the London
Community Gospel Choir and the Loyola Preparatory
Boys Choir, in a nod to his dual Spanish and British
heritage John Galliano had also been 'inspired by
his personal travels in Andalusia to invite numerous
Spanish artists from the Cristina Heeren Foundation,
including Manuel Lombo, Rafaela Reyes and the
Mariquilla to create a *fête* graced by their singing
and dancing' and to add a live flamenco soundtrack
to the collection, before taking his bow in a beaded
matador suit.

An Englishman in Paris

Unfolding to the sound of Sting's 'Englishman
in New York', the ready-to-wear ensembles
John Galliano delivered for the house after
the haute couture extravaganza of the previous
collection (see p. 448) revisited some of the hallmarks
of his version of the Dior style, as developed since
he was appointed creative director in 1997.

With a retro feel and a nod to Old Hollywood
glamour in the continuation of his recent collections
for the house, 'under the guise of 1920s-through-1940s
styling, he brought back his pantsuits as pinstripe
three-pieces and Marlene Dietrich white-tie tailcoats,
reprised the pagoda-shouldered silhouettes of his
Madame Butterfly collection [see p. 438], and, of
course, laid on a rendering of his signature bias
cutting in jazz-age chiffon and 1930s charmeuse,'
Vogue reported.

Madame X Meets Klimt

'John Singer Sargent's infamous 1884 portrait of [Virginie] Amélie Gautreau known as *Madame X* is the starting point for a journey of seduction,' read the collection notes. 'The painting of the society beauty, which scandalised Paris with its shocking combination of chic and eroticism, reveals the interest of *fin de siècle* artists in the symbolic potential of painting.'

'The perfection and restrained rigour of Sargent's art echoes the precision of the cut and silhouette created by Monsieur Dior, while the colours and ornamentations are inspired by the work of the Symbolists.'

Almost every outfit in the collection was cut from brightly coloured silk, then lavishly embroidered – extraordinary craftsmanship gave life to motifs inspired notably by the work of painter Gustav Klimt, while the designer used 'lots of volume to dramatic effect in exaggerated peplums, trapezes and pleated panels,' *Women's Wear Daily* reported.

With Led Zeppelin's 1969 hit 'Whole Lotta Love' as its soundtrack, the collection was accessorized with gleaming headpieces 'inspired by Diana Vreeland's *Vogue*,' Galliano explained (Vreeland was editor-in-chief of the magazine from 1963 until 1971). 'In the end, something in the odd air of high-society 1960s hauteur came over as surprisingly chic,' *Vogue*'s Sarah Mower concluded.

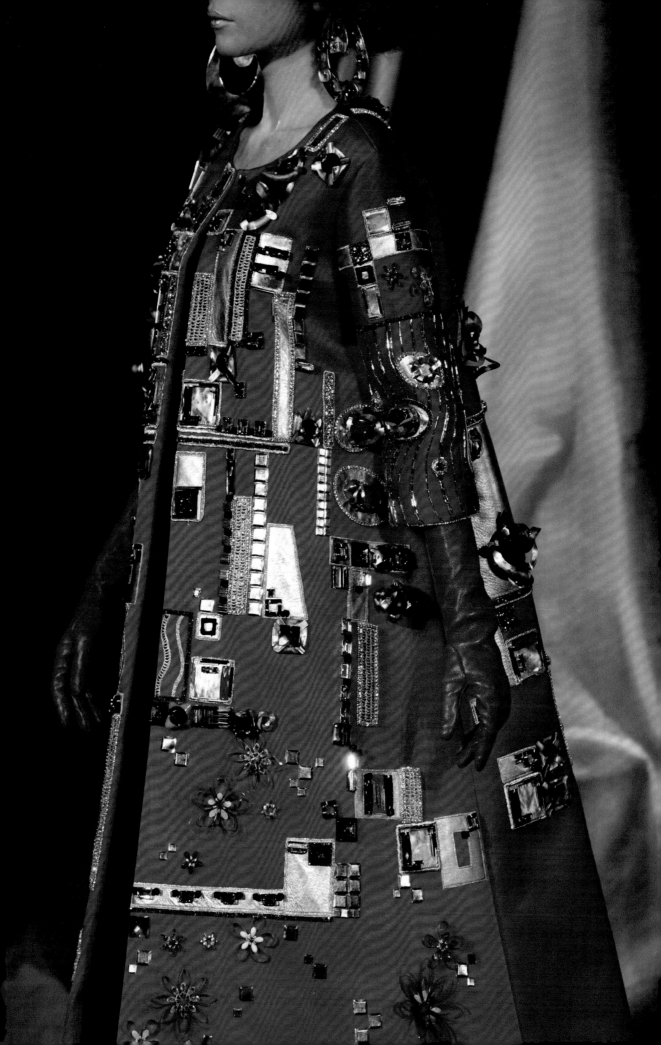

Celebrating the 1960s

Opening to the sound of Simon & Garfunkel's 'Mrs Robinson' (before moving to Dusty Springfield, another icon of the decade), this collection was a joyous ode to the style of the 1960s, marking the launch of a new handbag baptized the '61'.

Reinterpreting the bright oranges, reds, lime and fuchsia tones and gleaming geometric embroidery of his previous collection for the house, also 1960s-infused (see p. 456), John Galliano revisited 'gigantic back-combed hairdos, equally gigantic eye makeup, and the neat ladylike suits and dresses beloved of Kennedy-era America,' *Vogue* reported.

'I'm always looking for heroines who make me dream,' Galliano said. For this collection, his muses included actress, model and Warhol superstar 'Baby' Jane Holzer, as well as Raquel Welch and, of course, Mrs Robinson in *The Graduate*. 'They inspired a Christian Dior collection Galliano called "pure glamour," one that worked the joyful, high-voltage side of restraint to near perfection,' *Women's Wear Daily* concluded.

Homage to Lisa Fonssagrives

John Galliano dedicated this haute couture
collection to Lisa Fonssagrives, the star fashion
model of the 1940s and 1950s who modelled the
creations of the greatest names in haute couture
and worked with the top photographers of her day
(she married Irving Penn in 1950).

Focusing on 'black & white, architectural cuts,
leather studs, cloche hats, translucent chiffon
dégradé, contemporary embroidery' and 'classic
Dior drapes, sheer and buttoned with a new twist,'
according to the show notes, the collection revolved
around the house's famous 'Bar' jacket, reinvented
here into a corset 'Bar' belt in patent or embroidered
leather. 'Deconstructed sounds disrespectful,'
Galliano told *Women's Wear Daily*. 'Let's just say
I've decontextualized [the jacket].'

Worn in contrasting black patent leather over a
cream wool coat in the opening look (opposite, top),
which was reminiscent of one of Gianfranco Ferré's
creations for the house (see p. 223), or embroidered
and cinched over a multicoloured silk dress, the belt
echoed the curves and padded hips of the original
1947 'Bar' jacket.

For the finale, richly embroidered 'Bar' corsets
were teamed with matching gravity-defying
evening dresses in tulle and crin. It's 'couture
in a contemporary way,' Galliano declared.
'A season of change, cut and sophistication.
There's a sexy new step in the salon.'

'Tribal Chic'

'Tribal Chic – studded, belted, dégradé' was
the stated theme for this collection – although
'it's a sideward glance, an abstraction of Africa,'
Galliano told *Women's Wear Daily*. 'It's never,
never literal.'

The striking 'Bar' corset of the preceding Dior
collection (see p. 464) was reworked here into python
or leather bustiers nipped in at the waist and worn
over flowing and transparent silk dresses, styled
with towering crimped hairdos and gold statuette
necklaces.

Vogue's Sarah Mower also detected a touch of
1980s Alaïa and Gaultier influence – 'John Galliano
had 1988 ... on his mind, too, judging by today's
collection, in which he cast his eye back to that
glamazonian era of corseted waists, pointy bras,
Lycra leggings, and body-conscious knitted dresses.'

Dutch & Flemish Masters

The haute couture collection billed as 'More Dior
than Dior' was 'inspired by the Flemish Painters
and the structure and cut developed by Mr Dior,'
stated the collection notes. 'The vibrant luminescent
colours of Vermeer are mixed with the posture
of Van Dyck's Flemish aristocrats. The savoir-faire
of Dior's ateliers is literally *tourné à l'envers* [turned
inside out]' to expose the secrets of the construction
of a Dior haute couture garment, with delicate
embroidery almost hidden on silk underskirts
lining vast, plain, textured skirts.

'I spent hours in the archives, examining the inside
of Dior's designs, subjecting them to an almost
forensic examination,' the designer told *The Telegraph*.
'It was like discovering a long-lost love letter which
declared a passion for clothes that are beautifully
and elegantly made. It is an art, which the craftsmen
and women perform with love and pride.'

'As for the 17th-century Dutch elements,' *Vogue*
reported, 'there were cross-laced corseted backs and
cartridge-paper scrolls standing out on hips', added
to blue-and-white Delftware tones, motifs featuring
the Dutch tulips, ample four-leaf-clover skirts and
twisted brush-stroke hats created by Stephen Jones.
'Architectural, luminous, iconic,' the house concluded.

Persian Miniatures

'The Orient was a great inspiration for Mr Dior
– he made a trip there – but sometimes I travel
in my mind,' John Galliano told *The New York Times*
to introduce an exotic collection that echoed the
1910s and 1920s Orientalism of couturier Paul Poiret.

'Persian miniatures and the rich decadence of
the Orientalists inspire a new look at Dior's codes.
The bar jacket is reinterpreted *"à l'envers"*,' stated
the programme notes. 'The classic wools and
pinstripes of Paris couture are cut in oriental
shapes. The New Look is juxtaposed with the
Orient in an ikat jacquard in signature Dior grey.'

'Luxury is rendered in double-faced cashmere,
ottoman wool and astrakhan, rich brocade adorned
with paisley cutwork and accessorised with tassel
belts. Cocktail jackets are softened with oriental
trousers luxuriously cut in rich satin and lamé',
while 'skillfully draped dresses in luminous jewel
colours are delicately embroidered in metal work
and stones'.

'Fever in the *cabine*!'

Titled *'C'est la fièvre de la cabine!'* ('fever in the *cabine*'
– the small dressing room where haute couture
models gathered to get ready and change before
and during shows), this haute couture collection,
shown in the house's avenue Montaigne salons,
was inspired by 'the iconic photographs of Monsieur
Dior with his favourite models in the *cabine* of the
Maison Dior' to endeavour to re-create 'the energy,
excitement and anticipation that surround a Dior
salon presentation'.

It was a way for Galliano to pay homage to the
house's original models – Lucky, Victoire, Alla and
the others. 'Mr Dior adored these girls who brought
his creations to life. Each look is in every way
individual, acted out as a character for the audience
of clients packed in the Grand Salon. All in fuchsia,
orange, citrus yellow, acid green, zebra or jaguar,
this is personality dressing.'

It was, Galliano said, 'as if the girls weren't ready,
and someone said, "Just go!"', allowing the designer
to reveal 'the layers, supports and underpinnings
that sculpted the iconic silhouettes of Mr Dior...
Their meticulous inner construction is on display,
as is the savoir faire of the haute couture ateliers.'

Inspiration also came from a 1954 jacket that
Christian Dior had created for Marlene Dietrich,
which Galliano discovered in the house's archives.
'It's a beautiful velvet bustier with garters attached,'
the designer explained. Intrigued, he 'did more
research and realized that together they had created
what was the original body: Marlene would attach
her jacket onto her stockings and then pull the
skirt on top, so she could make shapes and she
could move and the line would be impeccable'.

'In this economic climate, I want to focus on
the established codes of Dior: the Bar jackets,
the panther, the lily of the valley,' he told
Women's Wear Daily.

Film Noir

'The shadowy world of *film noir* cinema creates
a new siren,' proclaimed the collection notes for
this ready-to-wear collection, whose lingerie-inspired
pieces were a direct continuation of the house's
previous haute couture show (see p. 482).

'The sharp austerity of a young Lauren Bacall, femme
fatale and client of Monsieur Dior, inspires daywear
in refined shades of nude, pale pink and beige. The
codes of Dior are applied to classic "Bogart" trenches
in glamorous lamé and styled with the new season
Dior attaché case.'

'Evocative and provocative, a new Arletty at the
Hôtel du Nord, the siren wears classic Dior jackets
in masculine pinstripes and Prince of Wales check
with lingerie', while evening dresses 'make an
entrance in rich fabrics from soft-focus pastels
to siren scarlet'.

'Dresses are seamed and panelled in delicate dégradé
transparencies of lamé, lace, tulle and chiffon, and
reveal the subtle "Illusion Slip" linings that capture
the sophisticated statement of semi-undressed allure.'

The Influence of Charles James

'I was reading that, actually, it was Charles James who influenced Monsieur Dior to come up with the New Look,' John Galliano told *Vogue*. 'And then I was looking at a photo of Charles James doing a fitting – and on the wall behind him was a picture of women riding side saddle. And that was it!'

'Charles James, and his *debut de siècle* ladies who rode *en amazone* (side saddle), inform the cut and asymmetric posture of the new Bar riding jackets,' the house stated, while 'halter-neck dresses and riding skirts are cut in Monsieur Dior's beloved classic English tailoring fabrics of red grain de poudre, fuchsia wool satin, tricotine, cotton piqué and tailoring checks.'

Both Dior and James 'shared a love for the iconic feminine silhouettes and illustrations of the "naughty nineties", as personified by the 1890s Gibson Girl,' read the collection notes. 'Tulle jackets, with asymmetric collars worn with softly draped skirts, are all rendered in fluffy textured embroideries of lace, ribbons and silk thread with layers of transparent tulle, organza and delicate lace in soft pastel colours of pink, pale yellow, and palest blue.'

'This bold femininity leads to the spirit of James's most infamous client and collector, Millicent Rogers. The eccentric heiress clashed daring coloured satins of magenta, petrol blue, olive and sapphire, all encrusted with heavy crystal embroideries, and adorned herself with oversized jewels.'

For evening, there were 'ladies in two-toned duchess-satin grand ball gowns shaded in the palette of Cecil Beaton's portraits – the expansive skirts are cut to evoke the gesture of the drape of a skirt when riding'.

Set against Michael Howells's dramatic backdrop of over three thousand white, pink and red roses, 'from *amazones* and dressage to his iconic ball gowns, we gaze at the influences behind Monsieur Dior's New Look,' John Galliano concluded.

'The Seduction of the Libertine'

Building on the equestrian theme of his previous collection for the house (see p. 490), John Galliano added a touch of decadence to the mix for this ready-to-wear collection, which he baptized 'The Seduction of the Libertine' (and introduced with a line by rakish 17th-century poet John Wilmot, 2nd Earl of Rochester: 'Since 'tis nature's law to change, constancy alone is strange').

'Riding in from the hunt that began at the haute couture, Dior discovers intrigue and inspiration in gallant riding habits as it goes from the stables to the seductive style, and verse, of those infamous romantics, the 18th-century libertines,' read the collection notes.

'Cavalry coats with blown-away collars are worn open over teasingly delicate mousseline and lace libertine shirtdresses, with twists of 18th-century floral prints. Textures ranging from aged leather to soft mohair, paperweight python to pony skin and punched leather mix effortlessly with chunky knits.'

'Classic English riding twills and tweeds, herringbones and an innovative weave check capture the mood set against an earthy, muted palette' for day, while the asymmetrically draped eveningwear is described as 'inspired by Delacroix'. 'This season, Dior takes up the heroic spirit of French Romanticism,' Galliano noted.

The 'Ligne Florale'

'Parrot tulips, crocuses, orchids, pansies, poppies and delicate sweet peas colour and shape a bold bouquet from Dior's garden' in this collection, inspired by Christian Dior's iconic 1953 'Tulip' line (see p. 62) and staged in the gardens of the Musée Rodin.

'I wanted to bring a bold new bloom into the salon and let the colour, texture and structure of flowers inspire a new beauty, and create the contemporary *Ligne Florale*,' declared John Galliano, who looked at Nick Knight's and Irving Penn's striking photographs of flowers as he was creating the collection.

In keeping with the designer's vision, 'rich saturated *dégradé* silks reflect nature's spectrum of colour', the house explained, while 'petal hems and floral-cut techniques skilfully crafted by the atelier ennoble vibrant shades of frayed bouclé, felt, tulles, braided mohair and taffetas'.

For evening, 'vivid hand-painted petal skirts, pleated tulle rose motifs and printed triple-layer organza gowns follow the precision and pigment of each floral reference to create a garden of new Dior beauties', cinched by raffia-like belts and topped by brightly coloured transparent 'hats' – playful riffs on florists' plastic wraps – created by Stephen Jones.

South Pacific

John Galliano transported the bright tones of
his floral collection (see p. 498) to a retro tropical
setting reminiscent of the 1958 *South Pacific* film
for this ready-to-wear collection (introduced in
the programme by 'queen of pin-ups' Bettie Page's
defiant quip: 'I was *never* the girl next door').

'The sun shines on the waterfront as Dior drops
anchor at a South Pacific naval base,' stated the
house. 'Tropical beauties mix masculine with
feminine as Dior combines sailors' uniforms
with the island's exotic charm to create a new
contemporary bird of paradise.'

'Peacoats and parkas in crisp white and navy
Nubuck leathers contrast with the rich prints of
hibiscus, orchids and palms of the South Pacific',
while 'nautical knits mix with reef-knot skirts, bold
sun-drenched cotton-print day dresses and sailor
pants styled with sarong twist silhouettes'.

For evening, 'floral prints and petal details with
the folds and knots of the nautical are lured into
a new adventure with lace insets and Galuchat
print. Midnight walks along the beach come in
exotic feathers, coral embroideries and shells-
and-organza garland belts.'

The Art of René Gruau

This haute couture collection was inspired by
the work of René Gruau, the legendary Franco-
Italian illustrator and friend of Christian Dior
who created some of the house's most memorable
advertisements in the 1940s and 1950s, from the
illustration for the house's first ever perfume, Miss
Dior, to the iconic 'Rouge Baiser' poster depicting
a woman wearing a black blindfold and bright red
Dior lipstick.

'Gruau's elegant drawings captured the essence
of Dior,' the house stated. 'Inspired by the
spontaneity of the illustrator's line, volumes and
movements create a fluid and elegant silhouette.
Dégradé tulle goes from light to dark as if handled
by a *chiaroscuro* painter, while the transparency
of silk organza and the bright colours of silk faille
evoke the intensity and the tones of the painter's
palette.'

'Lines were as crisp and definitive as a strike of
a pen on paper – they drew powerful, exaggerated
shapes like haute caricatures,' *Women's Wear Daily*
reported, while 'New Look references abounded
in proportions that made up for every fabric ration
ever issued'.

Describing the collection as his most technically
challenging to date, John Galliano (who originally
went to Central Saint Martins to study fashion
illustration) draped black tulle on his models
to evoke the shadows of both graphite traces
and Irving Penn's classic fashion photographs,
and topped his looks with 'strokes of paint'
headpieces designed by Stephen Jones.

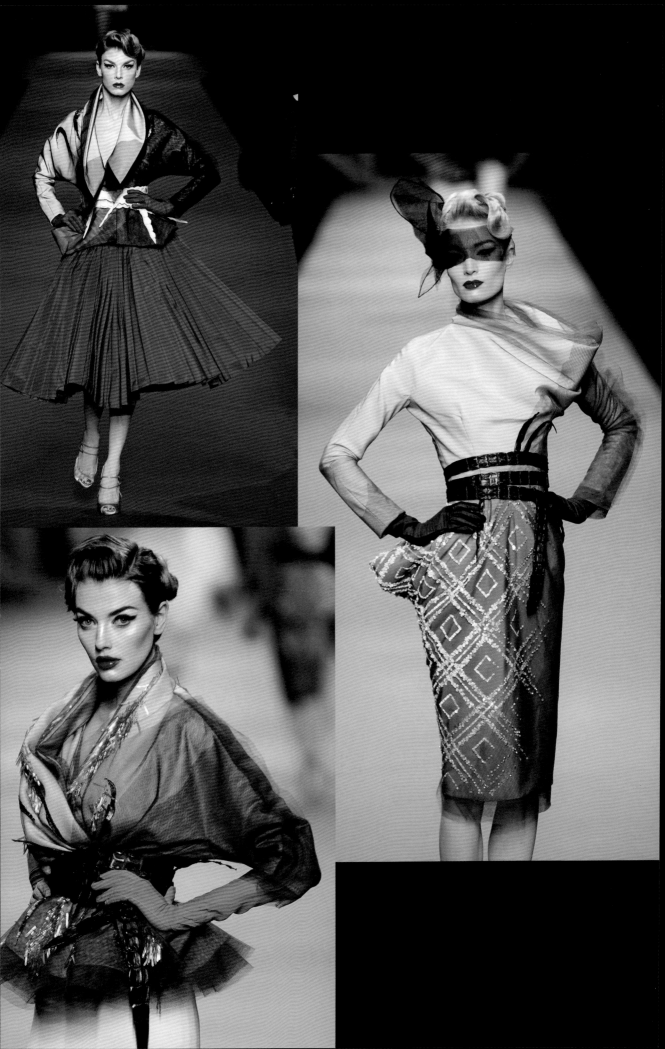

English Romantics

Presented at the Musée Rodin shortly after
John Galliano's dismissal from Dior, this was
the designer's final collection for the house.

'Dior's new silhouette for autumn-winter 2011 is
created by the maxi cape and coat, the knickerbocker
and the Dior Mitzah tee,' read the collection notes.
'The layered silhouette evokes the dandyism of the
English romantic poets. Rich inky shades, *changeant*
velvets, cashmeres, chiffons and organza create
a palette of textures and colours. Soft leathers,
suedes and furs, intricate luxe weaves, tapestry-
work and knitwear complete the look for day.'

Karlie Kloss, opening the show in a floor-length
cashmere cloak, velvet knickerbockers and
knee-high boots (right), 'could have been a female
Byron or a highwaywoman – either way, a romantic
renegade has always been the quintessential
Galliano woman,' wrote Tim Blanks.

For eveningwear, 'embroidery, feathers, tulle
and lace cut a new lyrical luxury'. As *Vogue*'s
Sarah Mower remarked, 'the pretty, dusty pastel
semi-sheer Empire dresses that walked out as
[Galliano's] final contribution to Christian Dior
just happened to hark back to the period of history
he explored in the *Les Incroyables* graduate collection
which first spotlit his talent.'

Bill Gaytten

A Steady Hand

A behind-the-scenes talent thrust into the limelight: the simplest way to
summarize Bill Gaytten's appointment to lead Christian Dior, in the wake
of John Galliano's dismissal in 2011. The easiest way to summarize his
reaction? A rueful quote from Gaytten himself: 'Dresses are designed
for the limelight, not designers.'

Gaytten steered Dior through one of the most tumultuous periods in
the house's then 65-year history – the aftermath of the departure of
creative director John Galliano, after almost 15 years at the helm. It was
an unprecedented crisis, seeing a key Paris house – a major world fashion
player – left rudderless at a key point in the industry calendar, namely the
staging of its autumn/winter 2011 ready-to-wear collection. That collection
had already been designed, albeit not finalized, by the time of Galliano's
dismissal on 1 March, so the 51-year-old Gaytten was responsible, initially,
for the staging of the show four days later (see p. 512), leading the design
team in the final preparations at the studio and also backstage. Later, as
head of the studio rather than as creative director, he presented two haute
couture and two ready-to-wear collections for the house – an interim
measure as rumours swirled as to the identity of the designer poised
to be appointed to the creative director post. 'Circumstances have been
forced upon me,' Gaytten declared in September 2011, prior to the first
ready-to-wear collection to be devised without Galliano's input since 1997.

Born in Cheltenham in the British countryside, Gaytten originally studied
architecture at University College, London, before being pulled into the
orbit of fashion. He shared a flat with a number of fashion students and
became enamoured with the work of past designers, including Dior, buying
a sewing machine and figuring out how to re-create historical garments.
Gaytten's technical proficiency – a combination of his love of fashion
and the construction knowledge gleaned from his architectural training –
launched a career collaborating with leading British designers. He worked
for a number, including royal couturier Victor Edelstein and Sheridan
Barnett, who had taught Galliano at Saint Martin's and who originally

introduced the two. Gaytten worked briefly with Galliano in 1985; after an interim period of three years, he returned in 1988, and stayed for another 23, working across the designer's eponymous label (of which he is now creative director) and also heading the studios of Givenchy and Christian Dior.

Gaytten himself is quiet, reserved and pale, somewhat delicate: he was the perfect foil for Galliano's flights of fantasy, both in his personal appearance and in his designs. Gaytten's quietness translated to his Dior collections, where the focus was on his own strengths as a technician, the wizard pattern-maker who had helped execute many of the key triumphs over fifteen years of Dior shows. Gaytten's stewardship of Dior focused, by and large, on technique: silhouettes stuck close to the suck-in, stick-out tradition of both Christian Dior and Galliano, with the 'Bar' jacket and billowing skirt playing key roles. Those recognizable silhouettes would be executed with unexpected materials and treatments, utilizing both Gaytten's prowess and the superlative skills of the Dior ateliers. The house's memorable spring/summer 2012 haute couture collection, for instance, presented dresses devised as 'X-rays' of Dior originals, exposing the layers of complicated construction necessary to form their extreme shapes. It also included embroideries that re-appliquéd crocodile scales, created sequin effects with ostrich hide, and traced evening dresses with roses based on embroidery placements, thus resembling plans rather than final decoration. Presented low-key and gracefully in the salons of 30 avenue Montaigne, it had a dignity.

Respectful, romantic and restrained are three words that summarize the difficult tightrope walk of Bill Gaytten's year-long term: respectful of both the fashion legacy of Galliano and Dior; romantic with an understated coquetry rather than theatrical passion; and restrained in both silhouette and palette. In fact, Gaytten's time at Dior was a much-needed palate cleanser, setting the scene for the house's next creative director, who would re-set Dior once again and make it look new for the twenty-first century.

Alexander Fury

'La Rose Moderne'
(Modern Rose)

A team led by Bill Gaytten, Galliano's long-time
right-hand pattern-cutter (joined here by Susanna
Venegas, Gaytten's first studio assistant), stepped
in to create the house's first haute couture collection
since Galliano's dismissal.

Entitled 'La Rose Moderne', the collection
drew inspiration from the worlds of design and
architecture, opening with a section that echoed
the vibrant motifs of the 1980s Memphis Group,
led by Ettore Sottsass.

'Sottsass inspires a bold pastel palette combined
with graphic black and white', while 'Dior roses mix
delicate petals in pleats, prints and folds of taffetas
with light gazar waves and triple layer organzas
with leather appliqué,' read the collection notes.
'Crisp clean lines contrast with a raw, hand-cut
finish while tutti-frutti embroideries pollinate colour.
Leather and plastic embroideries bounce high gloss
into newly draped techniques.'

After the Memphis moment, 'Frank Gehry inspires
shimmering soft metallics with glass sequins…
Modern waves are constructed in light *millefeuille*
forms of natural beauty, frayed iridescent lamé
and muted taffetas.'

Finally, Art Deco interior designers Jean-Michel
Frank and Jean Dunand were referenced as the
spirits behind 'wood and malachite prints with
sequins', while Marc Bohan 'inspires multi-coloured
rose petals on hand-painted chiffons' and the finale
set out to evoke 'Jean-Paul Goude [and] a night
at Le Palace'.

Postmodern Bar

Revisiting the graphic motifs of the preceding
haute couture collection (see p. 516), which paid
homage to the work of the Memphis movement
(the post-modern 1980s design group led by
Ettore Sottsass), Bill Gaytten's first ready-to-wear
collection for the house reworked the proportions
of the famous 'Bar' jacket.

'A dressed-up mood ran through the entire
collection, not simply the gazar and organza
that so many of the outfits were cut from, but
the classic Bar jacket, modernized with a wider
neckline,' Tim Blanks reported for *Vogue*.

'Inspired by the iconic *basque* of the Dior Bar
jacket, elegant proportions are revisited and
refined,' the house stated. 'Tailoring takes its
cue from Monsieur Dior's dropped kimono sleeve,
reinventing classic Dior silhouettes with a raised
waist line and wider neckline, defining a more
compact, current shape', while 'graphic construction
cuts throughout the collection in bold geometric
prints, stark blacks and whites in herringbone
raffia, and window-pane checks'.

Elegance X-rayed

'Elegance must be the right combination of
distinction, naturalness, care and simplicity' –
the line, by Christian Dior himself, headed the
programme of this haute couture collection, which
was inspired by X-rays of the couturier's creations.

'The collection is informed by photographic
opposites creating a luminous work in progress,'
the house stated. 'Jupons are finished with precision
as the semi-sheer layers reveal the exactitude and
construction behind each creation.'

'Embroidery is mirrored from black to white,
white to black, with a restrained colour palette
of black, white, and Dior grey... Cutting technique
is seen through translucent layers of organdie, plissé
and jacquard. Fine threadwork padding stitches
and semi-embroidered layers reveal the couturier's
precision, handiwork and the artistry of Dior
couture.'

For evening, Christian Dior's 'grand ball-gowns are
given a contemporary X-ray treatment of inverted
negatives and positives using dramatic silhouettes
of black shadow with white to create a modern
ethereal beauty'.

'Rounded Femininity'

'Bill Gaytten's ready-to-wear collection felt like
a quiet re-endorsement of the brand's DNA today,'
Vogue reported. Unfolding against a soft Dior-grey
background, 'pure shapes are given a rounded
femininity, playing with texture and tone to
create a contemporary, luxurious silhouette,'
the house stated.

'Dior's masculine tailoring codes are mixed
with a ballet femininity,' read the collection notes.
'Houndstooth is reworked with re-embroidered
leather ribbon and paired with layered organzas
and gazars. Gentlemen's tailoring fabrics in "faux
noirs" tones are pieced with leather and satin-
leather.'

'Severe draped cutting, integral to the Dior jacket,
is paired with a new, longer length skirt, both pleated
and semi-structured', while evening pieces reworked
'the purity of Mr Dior's structural gowns, re-cut with
sheer panelling in a palette of blushed nudes and
almost black, inky jewel tones'.

Raf Simons

The Modernist

What is 'new'? That seems to be the question the designer Raf Simons was preoccupied with during his three-year leadership of Christian Dior's womenswear. How to make Dior's legacy not only look new, but feel new, too?

Ideologically, Simons is a modernist – plugged into the immediate landscape of contemporary art and music, inspired by subcultures and youthful rebellion. In fact, his influences are, on the surface, more akin to those espoused by the radical Yves Saint Laurent than the bourgeois Monsieur Dior. Simons has his own namesake label – an innovative menswear line, founded in 1995 – to explore these ideas.

Yet there is an affinity between Simons's fixations and those that obsessed Monsieur Dior. Look at the New Look – clothes that captured the aspirations and tensions of a post-war fashion industry looking to make women dream again. They were a profound and pertinent reaction to the times in which they were created, just like Simons's own 2002 collection, inspired by the riots around the G8 summit. A different look – a different gender, even – but the same sense of encapsulating the moment, of embedding fashion in a larger cultural consciousness. That is what makes Raf Simons's work at Dior seem new, modern: the notion of capturing a sense of the time in which we live, filtered through the heritage of Dior, but resolutely contemporary. 'I'm trying to bring a lot of reality to Dior,' Simons said, 'which relates to how women live their lives today.'

Simons was born in a small town, Neerpelt, in Belgium, in 1968. He studied industrial design, rather than fashion, the pragmatism of which tinges his approach to clothing. He was initially interested in contemporary art, rather than fashion, mirroring Christian Dior's own passions. It was after watching a 1990 show by the Belgian deconstructionist designer Martin Margiela – known for creating clothes from unexpected, often second-hand fabrics, he staged said show in a children's playground rather than a salon – that Simons was drawn into the world of fashion. Margiela's clothes demonstrated that there was something beyond glamour and parties in fashion; that it

could connect on an emotional and intellectual level, equivalent to art.
This realization led to Simons founding his line. He first began to design
womenswear true in 2005, creating ready-to-wear for the German label
Jil Sander, in line with the founder's minimalist signatures.

Simons's menswear had been lauded as revolutionary and era-defining;
his womenswear proved just as pivotal. A powerful sequence of collections
at Sander closed his seven-year creative directorship: they traded on the
aesthetics of mid-century haute couture, but reinterpreted in saturated
neon colours and airy synthetics (better to take the intensity of dye).
These collections were widely influential across fashion as a whole; they
also acted as a striking dress rehearsal for Simons's debut at Dior, the
autumn/winter 2012 haute couture.

The word most often used to describe Simons's vision for Dior is
'modern'. Simons's feel for the forward-thinking melded with Dior's
inherently backwards-glancing romanticism to form a dynamic fusion.
Inherent in that is the sense of 'updating' Dior's creations: Simons's debut
Dior show coupled the sinuous silhouette of the 'Bar' jacket with slender
trousers, as if combining the legacies of the house's two great revolutionaries,
Christian Dior himself and Yves Saint Laurent (the designer who brought
the trouser suit to haute couture in the sixties). Other styles were based
on Dior ball gowns, abbreviated at the hip to form brief bustiers above
more slender trousers. Frédéric Tcheng's documentary film *Dior and I*
captured the process of the creation of this collection: it shows Simons
toying with garments from Dior's archives, including the *tailleur* 'Bar', and
a geometric beaded dress from 1952, named 'Esther', both of which wound
up, in some form or another, in the show. Simons wasn't interested in
reproducing, but in reinterpreting – 'remixing', to borrow a twenty-first-
century parlance – to give the clothes relevance for now.

That is the literal example – of Simons hands-on with Dior creations
past. But conceptually it was what Simons sought to do at the house
also: he utilized its well-established codes to a different effect – to create
a new look. Raf Simons found a modernity, hidden in Dior's archives.

Alexander Fury

New 'Flower Women'

For his first Dior collection (whose creation was captured in Frédéric Tcheng's *Dior and I* documentary film), Belgian designer Raf Simons looked to the clothes created by Christian Dior himself for inspiration.

'Mr Dior was a supreme architect of pattern,' Simons said. 'He could construct something so perfect and yet he would often throw in a gesture on purpose to break that perfection. He would make what he did human for the wearer. You could tell he loved women in that way, in that incredible gestural way.'

Simons set out to 'take the codes of Mr Dior and transpose them to make the haute couture dynamic', with an emphasis on 'the architectural symbolism of the Bar suit … [shifting] the jacket's construction into other garments,' the collection notes stated.

The designer's Dior debut was set in a grandiose *hôtel particulier* on the avenue d'Iéna, where walls had been covered with hundreds of thousands of fresh flowers (from white orchids and pink peonies to blue delphiniums and yellow mimosa), whose colours and 'architecture' were echoed in the clothes, creating new Dior 'Flower Women' (the way Mr Dior himself referred to his 'New Look' silhouettes and attitude, paying tribute to his flower obsession).

'Perhaps the contemporary flower woman is seen at her clearest in the dissected ball-gown silhouettes,' the house explained. 'Starting with the pattern of a ball-gown from the archives, the original silhouette is sliced and shortened to form a short dress or a top to be worn with simple black cigarette trousers. The upper half of the silhouette remains the same, untouched, the bottom half stresses the way we live now.'

After the black wool tuxedo 'Bar' jacket that opened the show (right) came embroidered cut-off ball-gown bustiers worn with tailored trousers (including a tulle creation embroidered with fuchsia velvet polka dots, see overleaf, inspired by the 'Esther' dress from Dior's autumn/winter 1952 collection), day and evening dresses with structured bustier insets, a striking 'Dior Red' cashmere 'Bar' coat (opposite) and an unexpected electric blue astrakhan fur bustier cocktail dress (overleaf).

Simons was keen to push for the development of new techniques and fabrics in couture, as demonstrated here through multicoloured mesh layered ensembles (see for example p. 534, right) and, most memorably, the subtle Sterling Ruby prints that were developed exclusively for the collection and turned into duchesse-satin coats and evening dresses (see pp. 531 and 534, bottom left). A splendid white organza dress embroidered with 'Pointillist' dégradé chiffon (see p. 535) closed the collection.

'Liberation'

For his first Dior ready-to-wear collection, Raf
Simons chose to 'explore the themes of liberation
both historical to the house and personal to himself,'
the house stated.

When Christian Dior founded his house and
presented his first collection in 1947, 'he embraced
the feminine, the complex and the emotional; an
idea of freedom from what had gone before,' Simons
explained. 'There was an idea of restriction and
then a psychological freeing up; the foundation
of the house is a reaction to restrictions. I wanted
to do that, too.'

Simons therefore set out to 'embrace the sexual,
emotional, sensual and feminine' – and the female
body – with this collection, which featured a series
of mini dresses (including short coatdresses inspired
by the 'Bar' suit) and 'crushed ball gowns worn
casually with shorts', described as 'cut-off ball-gowns'
in continuation of Simons's previous collection for
the house (see p. 528).

The designer also continued to revisit Christian
Dior's most famous creations: 'The Bar jacket
goes through many permutations, as do the
'A Line' [see p. 82] and 'H Line' [see p. 74] jackets
in the collection; pleats are inserted architecturally,
godets flare and give freedom of movement,
embroidery and appliqué appear in bursts,'
read the collection notes.

There were double-face printed pleated dresses
worn with black wool shorts, embroidered black
tulle and silk 'A-line' dresses, and a wide range of
metallic hues, from mini organza dresses to the finale
of voluminous printed duchesse-satin iridescent silk
skirts worn with simple black silk and cashmere tops
(see opposite, top right) that echoed Simons's first
haute couture collection for the house (see p. 532).

Spring in the Garden

Raf Simons invited guests into a new Dior garden,
created by Martin Wirtz (son of Belgian landscape
architect Jacques Wirtz) and installed in the Jardin
des Tuileries in the heart of Paris. 'I wanted to
do a very self-explanatory collection this season,'
Simons explained. 'I wanted it to literally be about
the season; to be about the very idea of spring.'

'The clothing and the women reflect the passing
of time of the season, beginning as the signs of
early life and blossoms from the winter ground to
the full flower and blooming of mid-summer,' stated
the collection notes. 'Much of this sense is achieved
through a concentration on the exquisite multi-
layered flower embroidery that increases as the
collection continues, eventually building to the full
flower of the balloon-backed dresses whose careful
construction belies a seemingly organic shape –
all ultimately controlled by the supreme craft of
the atelier.'

'There is a sense of the collection growing and
changing from where we started with the couture
last season,' said Simons. 'Yet still always with
a sense of continuity and reality for the wearer.'

Embroidered bustier dresses abounded – *Vogue*'s
Hamish Bowles praised the designer's use of
'three-dimensional foliate embroideries with a
light touch, clustering fine silk petals on a peplum,
or scattering meadow flowers over a black net
bustier' – while 'symmetry is eschewed; layering
is embraced, with silhouettes seemingly growing
in stages,' the house declared.

After black tuxedos and lamé or mille-feuille
(three-layered) bustier dresses came a finale of
show-stopping ball dresses, including a pale pink
and white bustier silk gown (p. 540, left) that would
be worn by actress Jennifer Lawrence to the 2013
Academy Awards (where she won the Best Actress
Oscar for her work in the film *Silver Linings Playbook*).

Warhol in the Clouds

Unfolding on a 'Magritte-style cloud path' that
meandered around the gigantic mirrored spheres
(an echo of Andy Warhol's 1966 *Silver Clouds*
installation) set up in the specially built space
on the place Vauban, next to the Invalides, this
collection brought together surrealism and pop
art, featuring as it did a unique collaboration with
The Andy Warhol Foundation for the Visual Arts.

'For me Warhol made so much sense,' Simons
explained. 'I was interested in the delicacy and
sensitivity in the early work he did; I was drawn
to that graphic style naturally in this collection.
It was that notion of hand work and personal
signature that fitted throughout.'

'This collection is more connected to passions
we share,' the designer continued. 'Like a real
interest in art – Christian Dior started his career
as a gallerist and represented both Dali and
Giacometti early on. The connection to certain
periods of time is also significant, his obsession
with the Belle Époque in his case, the Mid-Century
Modern in mine.'

Warhol's early hand-drawn work recurred throughout
the collection, printed or embroidered on dresses,
skirts and even handbags, illustrating the principle,
stated in the show notes, that 'the collection
functions in the form of a visual scrapbook, a collage
of clothing containing significant moments in time
both for Raf Simons and the house of Christian Dior'.

The 'Bar' jacket was reinvented in wool denim and
teamed with Oxford bags; Dior's iconic houndstooth
motif was 'explored and transposed, emerging
frequently as a wool bustier'; and Simons revisited
Christian Dior classics, notably with the striking
red wool 'Arizona 1948' coat (opposite, top left) and
the 'Opéra Bouffe 1956' bustier dress rendered here
in black leather (overleaf).

'A notion of asymmetry, begun in the haute couture
collection, can be seen throughout, resulting in an
abundance of permutations in the silhouettes that
can go from short to long in one look. The collection
is full of unexpected juxtapositions and visual
non sequitur[s]; a free association, like a personal
scrapbook ... culminating in what Simons refers
to as "memory dresses" ... embroidered and
appliquéd with motifs that point to parts of the
personal history of Dior.'

'Lace and energy'

Dior travelled to Monaco for the presentation of
Raf Simons's first cruise collection for the house.
'The sea front of Monte Carlo is the setting for the
show, a dynamic strip of sea that the silhouettes
glide by in the open-sided, streamlined simplicity
of the venue,' announced the collection notes.
'Here, the mid-century colour combinations of the
collection and the essential movement of the clothes
are highlighted in the Mediterranean light.'

'The focus for me here was on lace and energy,'
Simons declared. 'It was a challenge; I never
worked with lace before. It was about transforming
the meaning of the material; not romantic, not
historical, not old, into something light, playful,
colourful and modern – with energy.'

'A sporting fusion of historical motifs and a
contemporary take on the Dior archive, with
an insouciant ease and light attitude to all,
is at the heart of the collection,' the house
stated, while 'the motif of lace [is] examined
in a multiplicity of ways and treatments; printed,
embroidered, bonded, glazed … pushing the
material to the extreme.'

The iconic 'Bar' line was also revisited, as were
the ample 'Corolla' skirts of Christian Dior's debuts,
'here reimagined and redefined; history cut through
with bomber jacket zips, expressed in new materials,
and layered with knitted "sunwear", itself a take on
scuba swimwear and traditional forms of bathing
costumes,' added the collection notes.

'[Simons] has always eulogized the movement
of Christian Dior's dresses, but here, at last, he
acknowledged the restriction of those original looks,
so there were zips everywhere. And aerodynamism.
And asymmetry,' reported Tim Blanks for *Vogue*,
praising 'a floaty, peachy sundress in a satiny twill
that wouldn't have gone amiss on Grace Kelly, but …
bifurcated … with a zip' (see opposite, top right).

The designer 'took the conventional notion of cruise
clothes and worked with it,' wrote Cathy Horyn for
The New York Times. 'In other words, he didn't depart
from the idea that these are clothes for playing and
relaxing… Many fashion houses are giving more play
to resort, but Mr. Simons is actually redefining this
segment of the business.'

World Couture

'It annoys me that couture is thought of as the circus clown of fashion,' Raf Simons told *Vogue*'s Sarah Mower. 'What interests me is to get down to a more psychological level, to think about individuality, and the cultures women live in.'

For this haute couture collection, split into four distinct realms (Europe, the Americas, Asia and Africa), the designer 'began by looking at women from different continents and cultures who wear couture; their personal style,' he explained. 'The collection evolved to be about Dior not just being about Paris and France, but about the rest of the world and how many fashion cultures impact on the house and on myself.'

Each of the four sections featured a distinctive approach. 'Europe' focused on 'the almost mythical status of "La Parisienne" and the intimate links with the history of the house of Dior'. 'The Americas' was 'bold, sporty, dynamic and graphic – here the flag holds particular, emotional sway,' stated the collection notes. 'Asia' featured 'clothing full of balance, tradition and purity – the architecture and intricate construction of garments is the predominant focus', while, finally, 'Africa' represented 'freedom, playfulness and effortless creativity; the personal style of the Maasai being a particular inspiration' (years after John Galliano's first collection for the house merged the aesthetic of the tribe with the Dior silhouette; see p. 260).

The global perspective of the collection also influenced the techniques used by the haute couture ateliers, who incorporated traditional methods such as Japanese *shibori* (the intricate binding and dyeing process that produces fabrics with distinct markings).

In keeping with the idea of multiple, individual viewpoints that animated the collection, four photographers – Patrick Demarchelier (for 'Europe'), Willy Vanderperre ('The Americas'), Paolo Roversi ('Asia') and Terry Richardson ('Africa') – were commissioned by Simons to 're-interpret and re-imagine the collection as the show happened'. Their images, photographed on their own sets backstage, were projected live on the white walls behind the catwalk – together with floral images that Simons had used in his first Dior couture show – to 'bring to visual culmination this new distinctly personal yet global view of haute couture,' the house explained.

'Genetically Modified'

Shown under a monumental scaffold ceiling from
which brightly coloured plants and flowers were
suspended, this collection revolved around 'the
idea of twisting, turning and pushing Dior, where
the lyrically romantic becomes dangerous; a beautiful
rose garden becomes poisonous,' Raf Simons declared.
'So much around Dior is about nature, and there is
the idea that you can't change nature. But I wanted
to change the very nature of things; that fashion
exists as a place of possibility, risk and change.'

Starting with the 'Bar' jacket (here cropped and cut
at the waist; right), 'classic concepts of clothing are
genetically modified, their DNA spliced or dissected
to form new silhouettes,' read the collection notes.
'Skirts and shorts are cross-pollinated; pleating
is used extensively and architecturally to evoke
new forms; knits are made feather light, yet strictly
structured; a new conception of the "hourglass"
silhouette is introduced.'

The collection was divided into three categories:
'Traveller' (signifying 'exploration, and often denoted
by the use of badges and insignia'), 'Transformer'
('the existing ideas of Dior transformed and moved
on') and 'Transporter' ('the most transgressive
element, interrupting the narrative of Dior with
its own story, quite literally in the case of the "text"
dresses' that featured slogans such as 'Alice Garden',
'Hyperrose' or 'Primrose Path').

'I wanted a sense this season of a particular group
of women, a distinct new tribe, sophisticated and
savage at the same time,' Simons said. 'I wanted
to feel that you wouldn't know quite where these
women were coming from and where they were
going to, that they exist in a new place of change
and possibility.'

'Feminine Craft'

'What is seen as the decidedly feminine craft of the
haute couture atelier, combined with the distinctly
personal relationships between creators and clients,
is celebrated this season,' stated the collection notes.

Held inside a white, hand-sculpted interior inspired
by the work of ceramicist Valentine Schlegel, the
show explored 'a personal, almost private and
unseen world of women'. 'The interior is a radical,
female gesture,' Raf Simons declared, 'and I wanted
the women who wear these clothes to feel that, too.'

'I see this collection as almost abstract,' the
designer explained. 'I wanted to focus on the idea
of intimacy around couture more than anything
else, the emotional experience of it; the relationship
between the clients, the salon, the women.'

Transparencies, embroidery and cutwork took
pride of place, playing on 'the ideas of the hidden,
the intimate and the exposed'. *Vogue*'s Mark Holgate
hailed the delicate and architectural '3-D floral
sequins bunched into circles and surrounded by yet
more organdie ... and the geometric gauzy leaves
built into a fabric as layered and as light as a
mille-feuille'.

Simons was keen to keep his haute couture collection
contemporary and dynamic, pairing several cocktail
and evening dresses with embroidered, flower-strewn
couture trainers (see overleaf).

Christian Dior loved movement in his clothes,
Simons told Tim Blanks, 'and I was wondering what
would have happened if he'd been in business twenty
or thirty years longer, when the 1960s happened,
when there was a literal movement in society'.

'City Lights'

'This season I wanted to propose a new woman,'
said Raf Simons. 'A woman with power and energy
in a very definite way. I wanted to pursue powerful
tailoring, to offer another reality, another function.
This season is less about the leisure of the garden
and more about the pace of the city. I am attracted
to the reality of the urban world and environment.'

Baptized 'City Lights', the collection set out
to celebrate 'the strength and power of the city
silhouette together with the women who wear it',
combining femininity with masculinity, the traditions
of men's tailoring with Dior's vision of the 'flower
woman'.

Masculine fabrics and tailoring peppered the
collection: 'peak lapels, double breasting and horn
buttons take the place of more traditional elements
of the feminine *tailleur*, while the *flou* utilises men's
shirting for dresses and nylon for a new form of
quilted canework [*cannage*] constructed into gowns,
with fluid, double-faced cashmere for cocktail attire'.

The bases of trainers (introduced by Simons into
his previous haute couture collection for the house;
see p. 554) were transformed into a new take on the
stiletto heel (see opposite, top right), while their laces
were transferred onto corseted laced overcoats and
'Bar' dresses (see opposite, bottom left).

'White Flag'

'America is a constant inspiration for me,' said
Raf Simons to introduce this new cruise collection,
presented in New York's Brooklyn Navy Yard, by the
banks of the East River. 'The pop culture, the energy,
the fluidity ... there is just something so alive here.
What I always like in America is that there is such
a melting pot of styles. But there is always a look –
a strong look. Whether it is uptown or downtown,
East or West coast, there is always a strength and
reality to how women dress here.'

Entitled 'White Flag', the collection had the silk
scarf – or the French *carré* [square] – as its leitmotif,
transforming this into the 'flag' of the collection:
'its pop iconography playfully explored, its
conservative, lady-like connotations exploded,
its sinuous, free-spirited sensibility embraced,'
read the collection notes.

Juxtaposing hard and soft, 'traditional, firm
couture constructions, based on those of the stock
mannequin, are combined and contrasted with the
silks in the collection, the rigidity of the bodices
often at play with the fluidity of sleeves and skirts'.

The *carré*'s shape influenced the construction of the
garments, while scarves' traditional hand-painted
patterning inspired decorative motifs on printed silks
throughout the collection. 'I wanted to explore print
without being too romantic about it,' the designer
told *Vogue*. 'I was surprised by how raw and artistic
some of the archival scarves were.'

'Providence'

Raf Simons summoned vast and varied sources of inspiration for this collection, baptized 'Providence', ranging from 18th-century court dress to astronauts' suits, and more in between.

'Eschewing strict historical accuracy and embracing an amalgamation in the imagination, the collection is nevertheless split into eight distinctly different sections, each a variation on a theme,' the show notes explained. 'The historical sprawl of the collection spans influences from the 18th century onwards; it takes in 18th-century French court attire of both sexes and similarly synthesises ideas from the uniforms of both cosmonauts and astronauts up until the present day – the astronaut is a symbol of exploration for Simons and flight a reoccurring leitmotif in the collection.'

'The theme and variation structure proceeds as follows: *Robe à la Française* – a variation on traditional dresses of the 18th century, an amalgam of styles mostly worn with panniers, lightened with new tulle structures [see right; opposite, below; and p. 565, bottom left]. *Flight à la Française*: Here the flight suit meets the traditional dress; bodices and embroidery transposed at times, zippers and silk taffeta utilised [overleaf, bottom right]. *1910s Linear*: Sinuous, long-line coats with an Edwardian origin, travelling through history. *Bodice meets Jacket*: The transposing of technical details, employed at the service of structural form; bodices become skirts, jackets become blouses... *Justaucorps and Gilets* [waistcoats]: Masculine "court coats" of the 18th century adapted for the feminine form [pp. 566 and 567, top left]. *1920s Liberated*: Loose, "flapper" lines of the 1920s reimagined in *tour de force* embroideries [p. 565, top left]. *Collar meets Bar*: The Dior archive at its most abstract and geometric; pure volumes and shapes originating from 1950 are elaborated on, highlighting Christian Dior's architectural purity of form [see p. 567, bottom left]. *Techniques, Pleats and Systems*: An approach to decoration where tradition and technology combine; traditional piping, [echoing] the systems of astronaut suiting [p. 567, right].'

'I was interested in the process of finding something extremely modern through something very historical; particularly through a juxtaposition of different themes,' Simons explained. 'The historical inspiration is not the justification of the collection, it isn't its entire meaning. What I was attracted to was an idea of architectural construction – that is a very Dior attitude – and how the foundations of one era are based on another, how the future is based on the past; that is what I found fascinating.'

'Providence (Extended Remix)'

'In the last haute couture collection and show,
I was interested in the process of finding something
extremely modern through something very historical,'
explained Raf Simons. 'For this collection I wanted
to continue; I thought there was more to explore.
By beginning with the ingredients and the
form language of the couture, but going further,
I wanted the ready-to-wear to feel more modern,
more dynamic, more real – I wanted it to be made
available to a wider audience.'

Titled 'Providence (Extended Remix)' to confirm
its link to Simons's previous haute couture
presentation for the house (see p. 562) and shown
at the Cour Carrée du Louvre under bright white
'space age' lights, the collection continued the
designer's exploration of 18th-century court dress,
and astronaut and cosmonaut 'flight' suits, while
'new "micro jacquards" take the form of a digital
grid, resonating with the traditional Dior *cannage*
quilting, itself elaborated on and transformed
in the leather goods,' stated the show notes.

'It was an idea of confronting what people now
think is an aesthetic that is modern – it felt more
modern to go to the far past, not the "modernised"
look of the last decade. The challenge was to bring
the attitude of contemporary reality to something
very historical; bringing easiness to something that
could be perceived as theatrical. It is the attitude
that matters,' Simons concluded.

'Esprit Dior Tokyo'

Many decades after Christian Dior first presented
an haute couture show in Japan (in 1953), Raf Simons
chose Tokyo for the presentation of his pre-fall
collection, held at the Kokugikan stadium, one
of Japan's top sumo-wrestling arenas.

'There is an audience, and appetite, for fashion
in Japan like no other,' the designer told Jo Ellison
for *The Financial Times*. 'It goes beyond the history
of the house – although there are close links
to Japan... I was inspired by the attitude of
the Japanese towards fashion and this collection
is a spin on the sartorial style of Tokyo. I wanted
to bring together the extremes; to look at the
glamorous, the practical and the architectural
in clothing.'

Playing with contrasts, Simons juxtaposed 'matt
and shine, evening and day, a subdued and masculine
colour palette placed alongside bold primaries, the
practical and rough hewn mixed with the hyper-
luxurious and refined'; 'all are defining features
of the collection,' stated the show notes.

Even the 'Lady Dior' bag was transformed into
extreme versions, 'blown up to giant, practical
proportions or made tiny and more decorative
with thick straps, this classic now fully embracing
the connotations of *kawaii*'.

Sequins were omnipresent, with sequin knits
'frequently mimicking their traditional, utilitarian
counterparts such as the cable, Aran and Fair Isle,
now flattened and made into high-shine patterns'
or used as 'layered undergarments and polo necks,
placed under more utilitarian and everyday
fabrications such as thick wools, washed leathers
and coated cottons'.

Covering long-sleeved tops worn under white
crochet dresses (opposite, top), mink-and-leather
creations (opposite, below left) or oversize patent
leather parkas, sequins were also woven into short
embroidered jacquard knitted wool dresses for
a glistening effect (opposite, below right).

'Moonage Daydream'

'I was always thinking of the future for so many
years and I was always anti-romanticising the
past, but the past can be beautiful, too,' Raf Simons
declared to introduce the collection he baptized
'Moonage Daydream' in homage to David Bowie.
'There is a sense of the romance of the 1950s,
with the experimentation of the 1960s and the
liberation of the 1970s in the collection – both in
its materialisation and attitude. But I really wanted
to express something that felt relevant for today,
learnt from then, from the point of view of now;
something wilder, more sexual, strange and certainly
more liberated.'

'Embracing a hallucinogenic amalgamation in the
imagination, periods of time are conflated, mixing
the traditional with the experimental in materials
and techniques,' stated the collection notes. Fabrics
and techniques also 'push the limits of the haute
couture ateliers', with 'richly layered guipure lace'
dresses (see pp. 574, right; 575, right; and 576, left)
sometimes embroidered with sequins (see p. 575,
bottom left) or worn under photo-printed plastic
shifts, gilets or opera coats (see right).

'New fastening systems in lacquered leather also
structure and decorate' (see p. 575, top left), and
multicoloured jacquard knitted bodysuits 'are worn
as a second skin as are vinyl boots in acid bright
colours' (see p. 574, left), while 'tour-de-force' white
silk pleated skirts embroidered with multicoloured
ribbons (see pp. 576, right, and 577) 'heighten this
sense of the decorative becoming the architecturally
structured in the collection'.

'The typical Dior "flower woman" is subverted
and liberated in the collection. Made unfamiliar,
futuristic, graphic and decisive in her encrusted
and dripping lace florals, tattoo bodysuits and
hyper-real plastic blossom prints, she is at once
exquisitely decorated and disruptive in her
mirrored, octagonal terrain of the show venue.'

'I wanted that feeling of a sensory overload both
in the collection and in the venue for the show,'
explained Simons. 'Something encrusted and
bejewelled alongside the shock of bright colour
and sensuality in the clothing with an architectural
structure and interior that has a similarly
disorientating feeling; somewhere you cannot
quite place where you are, or which period of
time you are in.'

'Animals'

Building on the motifs developed in his previous
collection for the house (p. 572; from graphic
knitted bodysuits and dresses to skin-tight boots),
Raf Simons baptized this collection 'Animals':
'instinctive and elegant, savage and sinister, the
natural and human come together, to make hybrid
forms of distinct decoration,' stated the show notes.

'I wanted the collection to deal with nature and
femininity in a different way,' said the designer.
'Away from the garden and the flower, to something
more liberated, darker and more sexual. This idea
had begun in the couture, but here there is more
wildness, savagery and overt masculinity in the way
a woman might present herself. The idea of animals
and an abstraction of their patterns became key;
none of them literal, more the invention of a new
species.'

Oversized masculine tailoring featured throughout
the collection, and 'rough masculine tweeds and
wool felt find more feminine forms in opera coats
and sinuous, long-line outerwear, asymmetrically
and revealingly slashed,' the house stated. Abstract
animal patterns acts as camouflage on short
bodysuits and dresses, while 'long vinyl boots
serve as a second skin' and 'pelts of Canadian
fox, part dyed, part natural, form sumptuous coats
or dresses, slashed and inset with dense tweed'.

'The collection moves from the garden of the
"*femme fleur*" towards what could be seen as
the terrain of the "*femme animale*". Present from
the first Christian Dior offering in 1947 – with
the designer's revolutionary use of leopard print
[see p. 24] – ... abstracted and contrasted in a
startling, hyper-natural colour palette, accessorised
with bags echoing the idea of a new, exotic species,
this contemporary expression of the classic animal
pattern subverts and celebrates its meaning at
the same time.'

Le Palais Bulles
(Bubble Palace)

Dior and Raf Simons chose the unique Palais
Bulles (Bubble Palace) in the south of France to
present the house's cruise collection. Perched on
the cliffs of Théoule-sur-Mer, the Palais was designed
by Hungarian 'habitology' architect Antti Lovag.
Having reputedly called the straight line 'an
aggression against nature' and found inspiration
in spherical Inuit and early human dwellings,
Lovag began this masterwork in 1975 for then-owner
Pierre Bernard, after whose death the organic,
bubble-shaped, multi-level terracotta house was
acquired by couturier (and former 'head of atelier
tailleur' to Mr Christian Dior) Pierre Cardin.

'In many ways it is a form of architecture you
cannot connect to another,' Raf Simons said.
'It is more human than rational; individual and
playful. It is a place that I have been fascinated
by for a number of years and I am so happy
to be able to show here.'

The designer adopted the Palais Bulles as a
'metaphor for the approach to the collection overall,'
the show notes explained, 'gaining inspiration from
the colours, textures and light of the natural world
of the Côte d'Azur, together with the style of the
people who have inhabited it'.

'A confluence of styles, patterns, textures and
techniques evoke the multi-layered world of the
South: the overall and the artist's smock, the bathing
costume and the bias-cut evening gown all sit easily
side-by-side', while a 'handmade' sensibility came into
play with 'the exploration of more "homespun" crafts
and traditional techniques, with the atelier's take on
crochet, smocking and patchworking'.

Net tops were layered over fluid short pleated
skirts, while the padding of the iconic 'Bar' jacket
was echoed on a rubber tweed knitted hot-pants
bodysuit (see right). 'Land, sky and seascapes find
form in collaged Lurex fabrics [see opposite, top left]
and furs are knitted to form more tapestry-like
structures that further abstract the organic world
in scarves and dresses.'

'The Garden of Earthly Delights'

Raf Simons took inspiration from the Old Masters of Flemish painting for this collection, named after Hieronymus Bosch's late 15th-century masterpiece, whose luminous shades of pink and green it echoed.

'I was intrigued by the idea of forbidden fruit [re-imagined here as glistening round objects scattered on the catwalk] and what that means now,' said the Belgian designer. 'The idea of purity and innocence versus luxury and decadence and how that is encapsulated by the idea of Dior's garden – no longer a flower garden but a sexual one. The original inspiration came from the Flemish Masters and their approach to painting,' Simons explained, as well as from Martin Margiela's deconstructed autumn/winter 1997 collection, with its one-armed and asymmetric garments layered (and in places pinned with pattern paper) to give the impression of being half-finished.

'The famous Dior *manteaux* show their similarities to the mantles of the late Middle Ages and to the gowns of the Belle Époque with a vast and dramatic utilization of silk taffeta,' stated the house. 'Meanwhile, the jewelry is at its most luxurious and expressive, finding itself as a new form of *cannage* [canework] chainmail to be worn as a vest over garments' (see pp. 588 and 589).

'The Flemish and the French influences come together in the dramatic, almost *impasto* gestures of drapery, the concentration on historical sleeves [some in fur on neoprene coats; see p. 588, bottom left], and the Impressionist and Pointillist application of patterns that are frequently hand-painted on the materials of the collection or made from intricate, cut feathers' (see pp. 586 and 587).

'I wanted that feeling of the sensuous and luxurious to be implicit within the collection,' said Simons. 'At the same time the innocent, gestural and personal should also be there – I have repeatedly been inspired by the gestural quality of Mr Dior's work. The historical impact is pulled back into reality and this, for me, is what makes something modern. The venue, in many ways, is like a Modernist, Pointillist church; it's the place where all of these concerns come together.'

'Horizon'

With a mountain of delphiniums in the background ('a flowered landslide can be seen in the Cour Carrée du Louvre, escaping the traditional bounds of the show venue and pouring inside and out; a soft, fluid landscape of the future,' read the collection notes), Raf Simons's last collection for Dior was entitled 'Horizon': 'a clean and clear naturalistic line of beauty, looking from the past into the expanse of the future'.

'It's a calm one, and very soft — away from the overdone,' the designer told *Vogue*'s Sarah Mower. 'I didn't want to embellish. So I was thinking about the South of France — rainbows and the simple things. And there's a bit of Victoriana: something of that film *Picnic at Hanging Rock*. With a slight sexual undertone of darkness.'

'I wanted the collection to have a purity to it,' he explained. 'There might be a simplicity in how the collection looks, but it is extremely complex in terms of technique. There are literal layers of the past, from the Victorian-style underwear layered under the transparent bias-cut dresses and the Bar jackets and rough knits, but for me it still all feels oddly futuristic and strangely romantic. Like this woman is about to travel through space and time.'

Models sported '47' choker necklaces in homage to the year Christian Dior launched his eponymous house and the New Look (see p. 592, bottom), and the traditional 'Bar' jacket was revisited with a more masculine edge and paired with 'lingerie' tops and shorts (see right), preceding a series of three-piece pinstriped trouser suits (see p. 592, top left).

Tailoring aside, 'the traditional, complex pleating techniques of the *flou* proliferate, finding form not only in dresses but in the fluttering hems of tailored jackets and parkas transformed in horizontal striped duchesse satin,' read the show notes. 'Sinuous, bias-cut transparent organdie dresses reveal delicate cotton cami-knickers and chemises that can also be layered with cropped, rough-hewn Shetland knits; the precise geometry in the cut of traditionally heavy historical sleeves is highlighted in feather-light transparencies set against flesh.'

The Studio

Collective Creativity

Fashion is seen as a solitary pursuit: we think of the designer as dictator, a singular arbiter of style. That was not true for Christian Dior, whose workrooms incubated talents including Pierre Cardin and Dior's future successor Yves Saint Laurent, and Dior himself had been a promising upstart at Lucien Lelong and Robert Piguet before founding his own *maison de couture*. And, despite the contemporary fetishization of the star designer, it is not true today.

A Dior collection, whether of 1947 or 2017, is the result of a vast array of hands – ateliers of craftspeople, studios of designers. In the aftermath of Raf Simons's departure in October 2015, the house of Christian Dior handed the reins to a collective, to the studio that had worked with Simons during his three years at the house. Their role was to continue in his vein, to ease the path for a new artistic director to join the label.

For this interim period of twelve months, spanning two haute couture and two ready-to-wear shows, the studio team was led by a pair of Swiss designers – 41-year-old Serge Ruffieux and 32-year-old Lucie Meier. Ruffieux had joined Dior under Galliano in 2008, advancing to become head of design for womenswear; Meier came from Louis Vuitton, where she worked for five years after a period with Nicolas Ghesquière at Balenciaga. Nevertheless, the house's identity under their joint leadership followed the lines laid out by Simons: a modernist reinterpretation of Christian Dior's timeless brand of femininity.

Rather than the revolution the New Look epitomized, this was a period of subtle growth and development, of restating house codes old and new. The studio's first catwalk collection, the spring/summer 2016 haute couture show, quoted aesthetic shorthand for Dior – the nipped-waist 'Bar' silhouette, of course, but joined with *panthère* prints and embroideries of lily of the valley, Monsieur Dior's favourite flower. Even the presentation of the label's 2017 *collection croisière* in Blenheim Palace harked back to Dior traditions: both Monsieur Dior and Yves Saint Laurent had shown collections in the same venue – in 1954 and 1958, respectively – while the collection itself made play with the fusions of French and British influences that often inspired Dior, and later John Galliano.

This era saw the house of Dior guided by many: by the duo of designers, and the half-dozen-strong team behind them, but also by the skills of the *petites mains,* the technicians who populate Dior's ateliers, some of whom have worked with Dior since the days of Marc Bohan. The premières at Dior, who lead the workrooms, are living connections to the history of Dior – its living heart.

Ruffieux and Meier were open about their admiration for and reference to the label's past, particularly in looking beyond the New Look. Their second haute couture collection, shown in July, included references to Marc Bohan's tenure at the house, as well as to the Art Brut creations of François-Xavier and Claude Lalanne, who collaborated with Christian Dior on the avenue Montaigne boutique windows in around 1955 and with Yves Saint Laurent in 1969. However, the overwhelming inspiration behind the show was the house of Dior itself. The collection was monochrome, the shades of Dior's 'Bar' suit, and of the black-and-white photography that delineates the house's defining decade under its founding designer. The team chose to present the collection in the haute couture salons of 30 avenue Montaigne, as did Dior himself, while the design of the clothing was an ode to the expertise – past and present – of the Dior ateliers.

In the absence of a singular artistic director, prior to the appointment of Maria Grazia Chiuri in July 2016, the collections of this period are the product of the house of Dior as a whole. They are an homage to the power of teamwork, the importance of the collective, and to the manifold visions inherent in the process of the creation of fashion, where many hands make light work.

Alexander Fury

Lilies of the Valley

The first haute couture collection to be presented
after Raf Simons's departure was created by Dior's
in-house studio team, led by Swiss designers Serge
Ruffieux and Lucie Meier, who set out to evoke
'the spontaneous, relaxed Parisienne of today' and
to channel modernity in a mirrored set installed
in the gardens of the Musée Rodin.

'Volumes are freestyle, the Bar jacket changes
appearance depending on whether it is worn closed
or loose; the shoulder is sensual, bare,' read the
collection notes. 'Symbols and charms, chance and
superstition define the collection's world. They are
worn embroidered on clothing, as a good-luck charm
or affixed to a necklace. Here is the bestiary beloved
of Monsieur Dior, as well as his good-luck tokens,
for the designer was a superstitious man with
absolute faith in his lucky star.'

'Knits stitched like lace, lily-of-the-valley embroidery
assembled in such a way that it seems to transform
into a panther motif, unexpected contrasts of texture
and cut: behind the modernity of this collection's
new attitude lies all the virtuosity of the savoir-faire
that lives inside the house's haute couture and
embroidery ateliers.'

'Accumulation and Trompe L'œil'

Presented on a futuristic catwalk raised within the Cour Carrée of the Louvre, this collection 'placed a focus on accumulation and trompe l'œil,' the house announced.

Asymmetric necklines, rich high-relief embroidery and a wealth of accessories (from the new 'DiorUmbrage' glasses, with lenses lightly tinted in an orange, green or blue leaf print, to multi-clip earrings and delicate rings 'dabbed with little barrettes and colored plexiglas, glass and rhinestones') set off the mostly black palette of the collection, whose key silhouette echoed that of the 1947 'Bar' jacket.

'The plant motifs of a knit clash with the embroidered flowers of a skirt, bags and jewelry are worn in multiples, and even the furs are given the mix-and-match treatment, fusing fox, chinchilla and mink,' stated the show notes. 'It's also a game of appearances: a contrasting rippling peplum sewn to a jacket collar has the look of a scarf, while the motif-enriched linings of a coat-dress imitate the hem of the skirt swishing beneath. Optical effects allude to the Trompe L'œil line designed by Christian Dior for summer 1949 [see p. 36].'

Blenheim Palace

Sixty-two years after Christian Dior presented
his first fashion show at Blenheim Palace to a royal
audience, followed by Yves Saint Laurent in 1958
(see p. 114), Dior returned to Oxfordshire for a
special cruise collection inspired by 'the post-war
high society's wardrobes' and 'the restlessness and
wanderlust that characterized the period: the urge
to travel, to discover the new,' stated the house.

'English country life is expressed via the tradition
of the hunt – its reflection in the decorative arts,
rather than its reality. Shots of red are evocative
of the hunting pink, rustic tweeds and crisp poplin
of country attire, while 19th-century equestrian
scenes are knitted into intricate pictorial jacquards
or fused into English country florals. Those
intermingle with rich devoré velvets and silks in
Asian and African prints, patterns and embroideries,
underscoring a mood of exploration, a curiosity about
the world, and a fundamentally English eccentricity
in dress,' read the collection notes.

Accessories were a particular focus, with silk scarves
attached to handbags (some of which were decorated
with an updated version of the Dior logo pattern;
see right), looped through buttonholes, or wrapped
around the wrist in the style of Mitzah Bricard,
Christian Dior's muse.

Black & White 'Bar'

Unveiled in the salons of the iconic 30 avenue
Montaigne, in the same building as Christian Dior's
original atelier, this collection was presented as a
'return to the source, the foundation of the house:
the ateliers'.

'The Bar suit, the essence of Dior, is the principal
inspiration ... the signature silhouette of hourglass
jacket and full skirt,' stated the press notes,
reinterpreted here strictly in black and white.
'The only colour, the single embellishment, is
sculptural gold embroidery, inspired by the works
of César and Claude Lalanne, a nod to Art Brut',
and echoed in the gilded panels of the salons.

Designers Lucie Meier and Serge Ruffieux 'began
with the skirt, experimenting with pleating and
draping in the evening dresses and long skirts', while
'their linings, layers of organza to add body, become
garments in their own right'. 'The New Look's
volumes are made lighter, more contemporary', and
'the jacket itself is deconstructed, either elongated
at the basque, or drawn in vertically and gathered,
adding animation and movement, a new look,
a Dior spirit.'

A few days after this presentation, Dior announced
the appointment of Maria Grazia Chiuri as artistic
director of women's haute couture, ready-to-wear
and accessory collections.

Maria Grazia Chiuri

Femininity and Feminism

The name Christian Dior is inextricably embedded in the feminine.
The house's trademark silhouette is the figure-of-eight, from which hands waft in and out – visual shorthand for 'woman'. The universe around Dior is also quintessentially female, given over to the haute couture clients and their *vendeuses,* to the seamstresses of the ateliers, to women crafting clothes for other women. During the time of Monsieur Dior, a powerful triumvirate of women – Mitzah Bricard, Marguerite Carré and Raymonde Zehnacker – influenced the *maître* so much in his creation that they were dubbed the 'three muses'. Dior himself termed them his 'mothers', underlining another fundamental feminine influence, that of his birth mother, the inspiration for the New Look. And yet, for 69 years, the house of Dior had been guided only by male designers, lending a masculine tone to this very feminine vocabulary.

In the twenty-first century, however, that has changed: in July 2016, Maria Grazia Chiuri, a 51-year-old Italian designer and the former co-creative director of Valentino, was the first woman to be appointed Dior's artistic director. Her aesthetic – as of writing, nascent, with only two collections created to her name – is nevertheless fundamentally informed by her identity as a modern working woman, a feminist and a mother. Just as with Dior, Chiuri's mother proved a formative influence: she was a seamstress, fostering in the young Maria Grazia a love of and fascination with fashion from her earliest childhood in Rome. Later, Chiuri worked for that city's two key fashion houses – first Fendi, then Valentino.

Chiuri emphasizes that her interest wasn't the glamour or fantasy of fashion, but the reality – the craft that sits at the heart of haute couture, a craft she witnessed as a child, watching her mother work. Today, however, Chiuri wishes to put that technique to the service both of beauty and politics. 'I strive to be attentive and to be open to the world and to create fashion that resembles the women of today,' she stated, of her debut Dior ready-to-wear show.

By its very nature, that collection achieved it: Maria Grazia Chiuri is the first artistic director in Dior's history to debut with a ready-to-wear line, reflecting the reality of clothes for the majority of women, as opposed to the dream-world spun by haute couture. In a similar fashion, Chiuri's collection was obsessed not with 'woman' as a singular, unobtainable ideal, but with 'women', in the plural. 'The message, really, is that there is not one kind of woman,' said Chiuri. And her Dior mixed styles culled from sportswear and eveningwear, casual and formal, the street and the salon, reflecting the multitude of interpretations of women today – *their* reality, not our fantasy.

'We should all be feminists' declared a T-shirt, worn above a skirt preciously beaded but worn with ease, in Chiuri's first show. Many cited the restriction of Dior's corseted and padded clothes as anti-feminist, but Dior's professed aim was, after wartime hardships, to make women dream again. In a sense, his New Look was about empowerment – idolizing women, elevating them through fashion. Those skirts gave a woman a certain importance, a space to call their own: the emphatic silhouette drew attention. Dior armoured his women against the demands of a new time, via the absolute power of the absolute feminine.

Chiuri's aesthetic argues for a plurality not just for women, but for Dior itself; a shift away from the house's signature 'Bar' silhouette. Monsieur Dior, she reasoned, only designed for a decade: she, however, drew from the many different eyes who had re-imagined Dior, bricolaging together their various riffs, references and interpretations, from Saint Laurent to Simons. She also mixed masculine with her feminine, drawing on the embroidered insect motifs devised by designer Hedi Slimane during his time as creative director of the menswear line, Dior Homme. Through Maria Grazia Chiuri's eyes and interpretation, it is once again possible to see Dior afresh – to look at the New Look, and see something new.

Alexander Fury

'Dio(r)evolution'

For her first Dior collection (the first to be imagined by a woman in the house's history), Italian designer Maria Grazia Chiuri declared that she set out 'to create fashion that resembles the women of today... Fashion that corresponds to their changing needs, freed from the stereotypical categories of "masculine/feminine", "young/not so young", "reason/emotion".'

The central theme she chose was fencing, 'a discipline in which the balance between thought and action, the harmony between mind and heart are essential,' Chiuri explained. 'The uniform of the female fencer is, with the exception of some special protections, the same as for a male fencer.'

The designer explored 'the form and shape of a silhouette that's contemporary, agile and Olympian; exhibiting an elite sporting elegance,' announced the press notes. The padding and corseting of the New Look were transformed here into strong, protective fencing jackets and 'un-oppressive' flesh-coloured bustiers worn under fluid, transparent dresses.

The iconic 'Bar' silhouette was revisited in a freer way: 'the white jacket, which accentuates the narrowness of the waist and volume of the hips, is worn over a white t-shirt [emblazoned with a programmatic 'Dio(r)evolution' slogan], while the black skirt is reinvented in tulle to give a peek at the knitted lingerie beneath,' the house stated (see p. 610, left).

Key to Chiuri's approach was the desire to look at the entire history of the brand, and the work of the designers who preceded her. 'Sometimes people believe that Dior is only Monsieur Dior, but Dior is a brand that is seventy years old,' she told Tim Blanks. 'There were incredible artists who worked in the house – Christian Dior was only ten years. After there was Saint Laurent, Marc Bohan, John Galliano – for my generation, John Galliano at Dior is a reference – but also Raf Simons, Slimane [for Dior Homme], and Gianfranco Ferré. So I decided to look at the brand in a different way – on the one hand I decided to look at it like a curator.'

The bee motif that decorated white trainers and shirts was borrowed from Hedi Slimane's collections for Dior Homme, for example, while a new slogan, 'J'Adior' was everywhere from black-and-white elastic straps to choker necklaces and pendant earrings (see p. 611, bottom right), and echoed John Galliano's own 'J'Adore Dior' T-shirts (see p. 344) and 'Adiorable' tattoo prints (see p. 391).

Christian Dior himself inspired the theme of rich and intricate eveningwear creations: 'his lucky charms such as the star, the heart and the four-leaf clover are sprinkled here and there, cosmic and horoscope elements are embroidered in silver on midnight blue tulle, while tarot symbols were reinterpreted in the colorful embroideries of the evening dresses that closed the show,' the house concluded.

Labyrinth

Marking the seventieth anniversary of the New Look
(see p. 24), Maria Grazia Chiuri's first haute couture
collection for the house offered the labyrinth as its
theme and setting. 'In the gardens of the Musée
Rodin, a striking quantity of boxwood hedging,
shrubs and bushes came together to make a modern
maze,' the house declared. Reflected in the mirrored
ceiling, the moss-covered catwalk meandered around
a large wishing tree decorated with hanging ribbons,
tarot cards and other talismans.

'Fascinated by the myriad of interpretations to which
this archetypal form has given rise over the ages,
[Chiuri] perceived her adventure into the heart of the
Dior world as being akin to entering a labyrinth, the
way sprinkled with the flowers, plants and allegorical
images that form part of the iconography of these
places but which, at the same time, reference the
imagination of Christian Dior,' announced the press
notes.

The collection opened with 'Esprit de Changement'
(right), a black wool and satin tuxedo-style trouser
suit with hooded 'Bar' jacket. Presented in its
original black and white tones, the iconic 1947 Bar
was 'deconstructed and reinvented, even as a cape'
and reinterpreted in soft, swirling organza pleats.

Evening dresses were created in delicate powdery
colours, embroidered with stars, hand-painted with
tarot symbols or animated by flowers 'pressed' inside
layers of tulle. The ecru fringe cocktail dress baptised
'Essence d'Herbier' (see p. 614, right) alone necessitated
1,900 hours of work – its floral raffia and thread
embroidery motif derived from a Christian Dior
original – yet still maintained a natural, organic
edge. 'For me, doing something poetic is to do luxury
embroidery in an unfinished way, to give a human
touch – a poetic touch,' the designer told Suzy Menkes.

For the finale, Chiuri 'imagined a splendid ball
straight out of a fairy-tale', stated the house. She
played on new themes – 'Croissant de Lune' with its
black velvet moon crescent on black and nude pleated
tulle (see p. 615, right); the finale ensemble and its
'unicorn' headpiece (p. 617, right) – and revisited Dior
classics, from Impressionistic garden-effect feather
embroidery (p. 616, right) to 'New Junon' (p. 617, top
left), a pared back re-invention of Christian Dior's
1949 'Junon' gown (see p. 41).

Accessories were equally whimsical. Claude Lalanne
'imagined that the flowers, brambles, and butterflies
of costume jewelry landed on bodies ready to spring
to life', the house explained, while Stephen Jones's 'hats
and masks bring an aspect of gothic phantasmagorical
with a punk edge' (designs including feather tiaras,
'punk' burnt-feather coiffures, 'hedgerow' headdresses,
and 'frozen trees' fashioned from the spines of ostrich
feathers – see p. 615, bottom left) to complement
Chiuri's 'secret garden'.

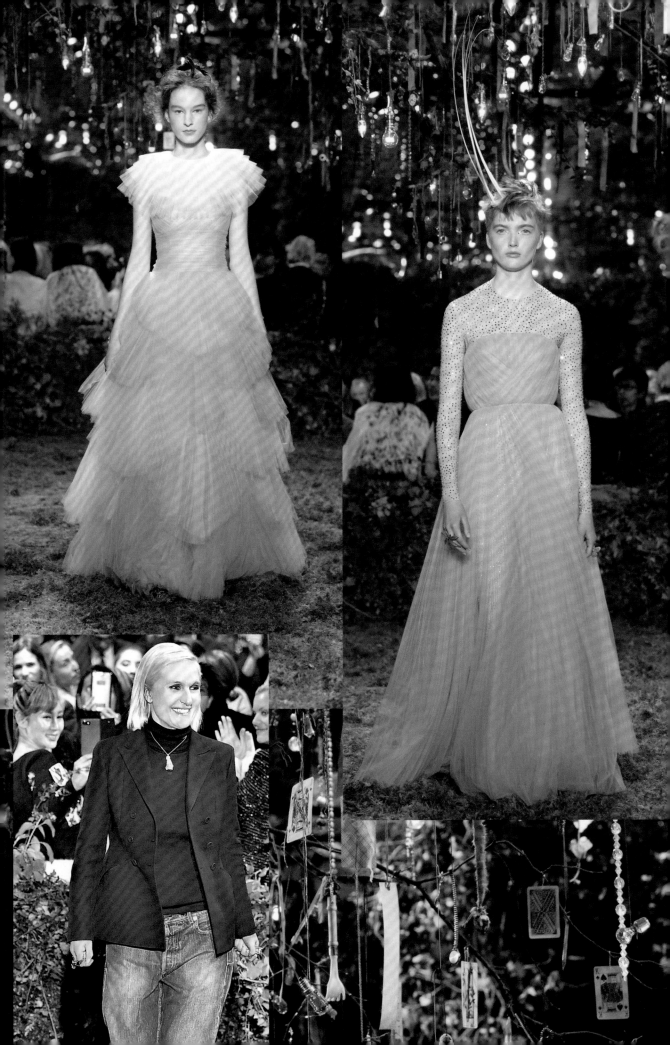

Bibliographic Note

In order not to disrupt the flow of reading, we have decided not to include references or footnotes in the main body of the text.

Sources for the quotations in the introduction, designer profiles and collection texts can be found below.

Andrew Bolton, 'John Galliano in conversation with Andrew Bolton', in *China: Through The Looking Glass*, New York: The Metropolitan Museum of Art, 2015

Christian Dior, *Dior by Dior: The Autobiography of Christian Dior*, London: V&A Publishing, 2015

Caroline Evans, *Fashion at the Edge: Spectacle, Modernity, and Deathliness*, New Haven: Yale University Press, 2003

Caroline Evans, 'John Galliano: Modernity and Spectacle', published on SHOWstudio, 2 March 2002 (http://showstudio.com/project/past_present_couture/essay, accessed 27 May 2016)

Alexander Fury, interview with Raf Simons, New York, 9 May 2014

John Galliano online: 'Dior Haute Couture Fall/Winter 2009–2010 Collection' (https://www.youtube.com/watch?v=duow2Q6u9qI, accessed 19 June 2016)

John Galliano online: 'John Galliano Explaining the Beauty of Dior' (https://www.youtube.com/watch?v=cNjXmIwIm8k, accessed 19 June 2016)

John Galliano online: 'The South Bank Show', January 1997 (https://www.youtube.com/watch?v=1dwhucghGJE, accessed 20 August 2016)

Bill Gaytten online Q&A, 16 December 2011: http://us.gallianostore.com/on/demandware.store/Sites-JGUS-Site/default/Diary-Show?fid=fashion, accessed 28 November 2016

Robin Givhan, *The Battle of Versailles*, New York: Flatiron Books, 2015

Cathy Horyn, 'More More More Dior', *System*, Issue No. 6 – Autumn/Winter 2015

Ulrich Lehmann, *Tigersprung: Fashion in Modernity*, London: MIT Press, 2001

Colin McDowell, in conversation with John Galliano for SHOWstudio's 'Past, Present & Couture' project (http://showstudio.com/project/past_present_couture/interview_transcripts, accessed 27 May 2016)

Glenn Alexander Magee, *The Hegel Dictionary*, London: A&C Black, 2010

Suzy Menkes, 'Ferré: Rigueur and Romance', *International Herald Tribune*, 24 July 1989

Sarah Mower, Review: Christian Dior spring/summer 2017, Vogue.com, 30 September 2016

'Cardin, Laroche, Givenchy Called Likely Successors; Dior: Fashion's Ten-Year Wonder Leaves Couture Leadership a Question', *The New York Times*, 25 October 1957

'Draft Date Nears for Dior Designer', *The New York Times*, 16 August 1960

Alexandra Palmer, *Dior: A New Look, A New Enterprise (1947–57)*, London: V&A Publishing, 2009

Marie-France Pochna, *Christian Dior*, New York: Assouline, 1996

Marie-France Pochna, *Christian Dior: The Man Who Made the World Look New*, London: Overlook, 2008

Alice Rawsthorn, *Yves Saint Laurent*, London: HarperCollins, 1996

Miles Socha, 'Paris Brings Double Duty for Gaytten', *Womenswear Daily*, 29 September 2011

Amy M. Spindler, 'Among Couture Debuts, Galliano's Is the Standout', *The New York Times*, 21 January 1997

NB: References to *Vogue* refer to the American edition of the magazine unless otherwise indicated.

Collection Credits

Marc Bohan

S/S 1980 HC – A/W 1980 HC:
Hair by Christophe-Carita

S/S 1982 HC – A/W 1987 HC:
Hair by Charles-Jacques Dessange

S/S 1988 HC – S/S 1989 HC:
Hair by Charles-Jacques Dessange;
makeup by Éliane Gouriou;
set by Philippe Astruc

Gianfranco Ferré

A/W 1989 HC – S/S 1990 HC:
Hair by Jean-Claude Gallon

A/W 1990 HC:
Hair by Patrick Alès

S/S 1991 HC, S/S 1992 HC,
S/S 1993 HC – A/W 1995 HC:
Hair by Aldo Coppola

John Galliano

S/S 1997 HC:
Hair by Odile Gilbert;
makeup by Stéphane Marais;
hats by Stephen Jones

A/W 1997 HC, S/S 1998 HC,
A/W 1998 HC:
Hair by Odile Gilbert;
makeup by Stéphane Marais;
hats by Stephen Jones;
set by Michael Howells

S/S 1998 RTW:
Hair by Odile Gilbert;
makeup by Stéphane Marais;
hats by Stephen Jones;
set by La Mode en Images

A/W 2000 HC,
S/S 2001 HC – S/S 2007 RTW:
Hair by Orlando Pita;
makeup by Pat McGrath;
hats by Stephen Jones;
produced by Bureau Betak

S/S 2007 HC – A/W 2011 RTW:
Hair by Orlando Pita;
makeup by Pat McGrath;
hats by Stephen Jones;
set by Michael Howells;
produced by Bureau Betak

Bill Gaytten

A/W 2011 HC:
Hair by Orlando Pita;
makeup by Pat McGrath;
hats by Stephen Jones;
set by Michael Howells;
produced by Bureau Betak

S/S 2012 HC – A/W 2012 RTW:
Hair by Orlando Pita;
makeup by Pat McGrath;
hats by Stephen Jones;
produced by Bureau Betak

Raf Simons

A/W 2012 HC – S/S 2013 HC:
Hair by Guido Palau;
makeup by Pat McGrath;
hats by Stephen Jones;
produced by Bureau Betak

A/W 2013 RTW – A/W 2014 RTW:
Hair by Guido Palau;
makeup by Pat McGrath;
produced by Bureau Betak

2015 Cruise – S/S 2016 RTW:
Hair by Guido Palau;
makeup by Peter Philips;
produced by Bureau Betak

The Studio

S/S 2016 HC – A/W 2016 HC:
Hair by Guido Palau;
makeup by Peter Philips;
produced by Bureau Betak

Maria Grazia Chiuri

S/S 2017 RTW – S/S 2017 HC:
Hair by Guido Palau;
makeup by Peter Philips;
produced by Bureau Betak

Credits included reflect the information
available at the time of publication.
We would be pleased to insert an appropriate
acknowledgment for missing credits in any
subsequent reprint.

Picture Credits

All images © firstVIEW
unless otherwise indicated.

Photo © AGIP/Bridgeman Images: 50, 51 (below), 55, 87, 114

British Pathé: 115, 116

© Catwalkpictures.com: 182, 183 (below), 197, 198, 200–1, 202–3, 204, 206–7, 208–9, 212–13, 214–15, 216, 217 (below), 218–19, 220 (below), 221, 222–23, 224–25, 226–27, 228–29, 230–31, 232, 233 (above left and below), 234–35, 236, 237 (above and below right), 239, 241 (above right), 242–43, 244–45, 583 (below)

Diomedia/Keystone Pictures USA: 69, 142, 173 (above left), 195 (right)

© Christian Dior: 24, 25, 39 (below), 40, 82, 94–5, 113, 123, 128–29, 166, 167 (above), 170, 171 (above and below), 186, 188–89, 191, 205, 609, 610 (below), 611 (left and above right), 612, 613 (above left, below left and above right), 614 (above left), 615 (above left and below right), 616 (above), 617 (above)

Courtesy of Christian Dior © Adrien Dirand: 2, 614-15 (background), 616 (below, background), 617 (below, background)

Les Editions Jalou, *L'Officiel*, 1952: 60

The Fashion Group International, Inc.: 138-41, 144-65, 168-69

Jean-Philippe Charbonnier/Gamma-Rapho: 45 (above), 111, 118–19, 120–21

Keystone-France/Gamma-Rapho: 173 (above right and below), 174–75, 178

Michel Ginfray/Gamma-Rapho: 183 (above and right)

Eugene Kammerman/Gamma-Rapho: 26

adoc-photos/Corbis via Getty Images: 72–3

Pool Arnal/Picot/Gamma-Rapho via Getty Images: 238

Bettmann/Getty Images: 54, 83

Walter Carone/*Paris Match* via Getty Images: 48–9

Jacques Dejean/Sygma via Getty Images: 172

Robert Doisneau/Gamma-Rapho/ Getty Images: 89

Pat English/The LIFE Picture Collection/ Getty Images: 27, 28, 29 (below)

Nat Farbman/The LIFE Picture Collection/ Getty Images: 52

Jack Garofalo/*Paris Match* via Getty Images: 66–7

Thurston Hopkins/Getty Images: 84–5

Maurice Jarnoux/*Paris Match* via Getty Images: 86

Mark Kauffman/The LIFE Premium Collection/ Getty Images: 30–31

Keystone-France/Gamma-Rapho via Getty Images: 51 (above), 53

Philippe Le Tellier/*Paris Match* via Getty Images: 96–7, 98–9, 100–1

Manuel Litran/*Paris Match* via Getty Images: 176, 177 (below)

OFF/AFP/Getty Images: 91

Popperfoto/Getty Images: 45 (below)

Bertrand Rindoff Petroff/Getty Images: 193

Willy Rizzo/*Paris Match* via Getty Images: 62–3, 64–5, 102–3, 104, 108–9, 110, 112, 117

Frank Scherschel/The LIFE Picture Collection/ Getty Images: 29 (above left)

Daniel Simon/Gamma-Rapho via Getty Images: 233 (above right)

Roger Wood/*Picture Post*/Getty Images: 59

Jean-Luce Huré: 184, 190, 192

La mode de printemps chez Christian Dior, 01/01/1954. © Institut National de l'Audiovisuel (INA): 70–71

Les Actualités Françaises – Mode de printemps: la nouvelle ligne selon Dior, 02/03/1960. © Institut National de l'Audiovisuel (INA): 124–25, 126–27

© Marc Riboud/Magnum Photos: 122

© Marilyn Silverstone/Magnum Photos: 105

Guy Marineau: 196

© Mark Shaw/mptvimages.com: 68, 74–5, 76–7, 78–9, 80–81, 132–33, 134–35, 136–37

AP/Press Association Images: 180

Pierre Godot/AP/Press Association Images: 143

Levy/AP/Press Association Images: 41, 194, 195 (left)

Jacques Marqueton/AP/Press Association Images: 171 (right), 179 (right), 181

Stevens/AP/Press Association Images: 199

Taylor/AP/Press Association Images: 185

Reginald Gray/REX/Shutterstock: 177 (above and right)

Roger-Viollet/REX/Shutterstock: 29 (above right)

© Association Willy Maywald/ADAGP, Paris and DACS, London 2017: 32–3, 34–5, 36–7, 38, 39 (above), 42–3, 44, 46–7, 56–7, 58, 61, 88, 90, 92–3

Topfoto: 167 (right and below)

Roger-Viollet/Topfoto: 187

The authors and the publisher would like to thank Olivier Bialobos, Jérôme Gautier, Soïzic Pfaff and Perrine Scherrer at Christian Dior for their assistance and support in the making of this book.

Additional thanks to Kerry Davis and Don Ashby at firstVIEW.

Select Index of Clothes, Accessories & Materials

The page numbers below refer to illustrations.

Accessories

Embellishments & Materials

Index of Models

The page numbers below refer to illustrations.

Considerable efforts have been made to identify
the models featured in this book, but in some
cases we have been unable to do so. We would be
pleased to insert an appropriate acknowledgment
in any subsequent reprint.

Index

First published in the United Kingdom
in 2017 by Thames & Hudson Ltd,
181A High Holborn, London WC1V 7QX

Reprinted 2021

Dior: The Complete Collections
© 2017 Thames & Hudson Ltd, London

Introduction and designer profiles
© 2017 Alexander Fury

Series concept and collections texts by Adélia Sabatini
© 2017 Thames & Hudson Ltd, London

Photographs © 2017 firstVIEW unless otherwise stated

Design by Fraser Muggeridge studio

All Rights Reserved. No part of this publication may be
reproduced or transmitted in any form or by any means,
electronic or mechanical, including photocopy, recording
or any other information storage and retrieval system,
without prior permission in writing from the publisher.

British Library Cataloguing-in-Publication Data
A catalogue record for this book is available from the
British Library

ISBN 978-0-500-51934-9

Printed and bound in China by
C&C Offset Printing Co. Ltd

MIX
Paper from
responsible sources
FSC® C008047

Be the first to know about our new releases,
exclusive content and author events by visiting
thamesandhudson.com
thamesandhudsonusa.com
thamesandhudson.com.au